A Matter of Faith

Praise for *A Matter of Faith*

The ever-ingenious creativity of our great God always amazes as my friend Joan Patterson can attest. With great credibility born of life-altering circumstance, her reliance on our good God in the midst of challenge coupled with the unusual manner He chose to meet her need through a service dog named Faith is both inspiring and encouraging. A solution born of the simplicity of His creation—isn't that just like our God to show up in the whisper?

—DR. PETER W. TEAGUE

President Emeritus

Lancaster Bible College

Capital Seminary & Graduate School

Heartwarming. Inspiring. Poignant. Words cannot adequately describe this story about a woman with MS and her service dog Faith. This is a book you'll want to share with friends. But be sure to insist they return it since you'll want to read it again and again. Better still, gift them with it. They will thank you.

—MARLENE BAGNULL

Write His Answer Ministries

Director, Philadelphia Christian Writers Conference

Director, Colorado Christian Writers Conference

It was my privilege to have Joan Patterson and her service dog Faith attending our *Lancaster Christian Writers* association. We often joked that Faith was our best-behaved member, and indeed the level of her disciplined, faithful service to her human partner amazed all of us. I can testify to the veracity of many hilarious, heartwarming, and inspiring adventures told in these pages. And to the testimony of faith and unconditional love Joan's relationship with both her heavenly Father and four-legged Faith proved for the rest of us. A delightful, inspiring read with the most loveable of protagonists.

—JEANETTE WINDLE

award-winning author *Veiled Freedom, Congo Dawn, All Saints*

CEO *JM Windle Editorial Services*

founder *Lancaster Christian Writers*

A touching story and inspiring journey from fear of change to a service dog named Faith to faith in God's direction!

—LAURA J. SHUE

York County Recorder of Deeds

A Matter of Faith

Surviving Life's Crises with Four Wheels, Four Paws, and a Loving God

Joan Patterson

Joan Patterson Publishing

Copyright-© 2022 Joan Patterson

ISBN (paperback) 979-8-9873693-0-2

ISBN (e-book) 979-8-9873693-1-9

Published by Joan Patterson Publishing, York PA

Edited by Jeanette Windle (www.jeanettewindle.com)

Karl Ceazar Arlegui (Fyra⏶ at www.99designs.com)

Book and Ebook interior design and format created by EBook Listing Services (www.ebooklistingservices.com)

Visit the author at www.joanpatterson.org

Publisher's Cataloging-in-Publication Data

Names: Patterson, Joan, author.Title: A matter of faith : surviving life's crises with four wheels , four paws , and a loving God / by Joan Patterson.
Description: York, PA: Joan Patterson Publishing, 2022.
Identifiers: LCCN: 2022922413 | ISBN: 979-8-9873693-0-2 (paperback) | 979-8-9873693-1-9 (ebook)
Subjects: LCSH Patterson, Joan. | People with disabilities--United States--Biography. | Service dogs. | Human-animal interactions. | Christian life. | BISAC BIOGRAPHY & AUTOBIOGRAPHY / Personal Memoirs | BIOGRAPHY & AUTOBIOGRAPHY / People with Disabilities | BIOGRAPHY & AUTOBIOGRAPHY / Religious | PETS / Essays & Narratives.
Classification: LCC HV3013.P38 2022 | DDC 362.4/092/2--dc23

Joan Patterson Publishing

Dedication

This book is dedicated to my loving husband **Chas**, who faithfully supported me through the long process, and to my dear mother **Arlene Ressler**, who at first thought a service dog would be too much for me to handle. She became my biggest supporter, bringing treats to my dog on a weekly basis and frequently asking when this book would be finished. She once commented, "I'll be dead before you get that book written." Sadly, she was correct.

Acknowledgements

So many people have helped along the way to make this project what it is. A special thanks and appreciation to the people at *Canine Partners for Life*, since without them there would be no book, including founder **Darlene Sullivan**, trainers **Megan Escherick** and **Deb Bauer**, and Faith's initial puppy raiser **Yuka Fujimoto**.

Various Christian writers conferences and the monthly *Lancaster Christian Writers* association all helped me hone my writing so people could understand what was written. Much thanks to **Marsha Hubler**, director of Montrose Christian Writers Conference, and **Marlene Bagnull**, director of Philadelphia Christian Writers Conference and Colorado Christian Writers Conference, who taught this fledging writer there is more to good writing than putting words on paper.

A huge thanks to bestselling author **Cecil Murphey**, who believed in me enough to help me attend writers conferences through scholarships and who taught me certain rules of the written word I still hear whispering in my ear when I write.

Another big thanks to my editor **Jeanette Windle**, who gently prodded and pushed me through the fourteen years it took to get this book where it is, and to **Amy Deardon** of www.EBookListing Services.com, who worked wonders to make the message on the inside look good on the outside.

Most of all I give all the glory and praise to **GOD**, the One who held my hand and kept me on track.

Table of Contents

Foreword

By Darlene Sullivan
Founder of Canine Partners for Life

Speaking of disability, particularly one's own, can be challenging. Many would prefer to hermit themselves away rather than be seen or speak of the challenges they face and their outward "differences" most others cannot fully understand. Likewise, publicly and openly describing one's faith journey can be daunting. Completing both tasks in a manner that will keep readers engaged, curious, and turning pages as they laugh, cry, widen their eyes, and nod heads in a new level of understanding is far from easy. But that is what Joan Patterson has accomplished with genuine honesty in her memoir *A Matter of Faith*.

Like all challenges in life, disability also brings blessings. But you must be wise enough to see them and open enough to accept them. In this narrative of her life journey, Joan has shared the feelings of grief and despair along with the yearning to search for answers that would help her be purposeful, useful, and competent.

She has struggled with acceptance and had to be creative in her many solutions.

Above all, she had to have faith. Faith in her heavenly Father and Faith that came in the four-legged, tail-wagging, furry form. Throughout these pages, you will see how her partnerships with both develop and grow. And as a result, how Joan finds answers, love, and purpose.

The four-legged Faith received her name long before she was partnered with Joan. But most certainly, her path had already been chosen and her purpose predetermined right down to the name given to her. As Joan and Faith in partnership with God learn to live a full life together, they embrace the reader as they embraced me so many years ago when Joan decided to take a risk and be partnered with a service dog.

Having founded the organization from which Joan received four-legged Faith and been privileged to guide them through the process of becoming a team, it has been a joy to see such growth. Especially having faced many of the same physical and faith challenges Joan has tackled. I can assure you the experiences she writes about in this book were as awful, hysterical, and heartwarming as shared. I was present for many of them, counseled Joan through any number, and learned from her experience and faith (the non-four-legged kind!) just as you will.

Strength is knowing yourself and accepting that God's design for you is intentional and purposeful. That if you have faith, He will always bring to you the resources you need. So as you read the

following pages, open your heart, feel, learn, laugh, and cry. Feel
Joan's strength and trust in God. Then use those lessons to live your
life and share with the world your own personal strength and faith.

Darlene Sullivan
Founder, Canine Partners for Life
Service Dog Trainer/Educator/Advocate

Introduction

*M*y life didn't always include a wheelchair. At least not until multiple sclerosis (MS) began to slow me down. Joy walked away as MS rolled in. My confidence faltered along with my faith that I could continue being a viable asset to society, much less care for my own family.

The MS diagnosis wasn't my first major health crisis. Fibrocystic breast disease eventually led to a full mastectomy. I'd also survived multiple bouts of kidney stones, some large, some small. A round of food poisoning frightened both me and my husband Chas. All painful but temporary. Multiple sclerosis wasn't painful, but it would stay with me the rest of my life.

My MS journey began at a particularly busy time. Raising two boys and being a teacher at the same school where my husband taught kept my schedule hectic. One day I noticed the left side of my face felt different as though Novocain from a dental procedure hadn't completely worn off. A visit to my doctor determined a pinched nerve in my neck. I got to relax several times a day while I donned a contraption which attached to my bed and wrapped around my head. It gave me time for short naps. It also didn't help.

Then my left arm became numb like my face. Now the doctor started looking concerned. Something was clearly going on other than a pinched nerve in my neck. Thus began a frustrating round of medical appointments. Doctor after doctor remarked that I had all the signs and symptoms of multiple sclerosis, but of course that couldn't be it since my MRI (magnetic resonance imaging) scan was clear. When one doctor finally determined I did have MS, the diagnosis was actually a relief. At least I now knew what was going on in my body.

Daily routines needed to be modified according to my energy level. Sometimes getting presentable for the day proceeded as usual. No problem dressing, combing my hair, or grabbing a quick breakfast. Other mornings my energy level was so low I couldn't get dressed without taking breaks to rest. My arm would be too weak to raise, so instead I brought my head down to my arm to brush and style my hair. On slow days, breakfast might be reduced to eating toast in the car while on my way to my teaching job.

Despite my MS, I still felt useful, whether teaching in a formal school setting or holding professional workshops, as I began to do. Instructing construction professionals about compliance with building accessibility according to the Americans with Disabilities Act (ADA), for instance, invigorated me. I was still contributing to society. The MS had affected my body but not my mind. Even when I changed occupations and became the local real estate tax collector for my area, I remained productive. Now work was done from home, and I could basically set my own schedule.

But as the years went by, my body progressively deteriorated. At first, I could walk wherever I wanted, though with a cane for stability. When my balance and energy level forced me to seek a different way to complete my day's chores, a three-wheeled scooter became my mode of transportation. Chores that involved major walking like grocery shopping could be completed only with the scooter. But in my judgment, a scooter was not a visible sign of being an invalid.

After wearing out my second scooter, I made an appointment to be fitted for another scooter. The representative arrived with both a scooter and power wheelchair. I don't know about you, but when I make up my mind about something, I vehemently refuse to change it. There was no way I was going to succumb to using such transportation as a wheelchair. Wheelchairs were for invalids. I wasn't bad off enough to need one.

Or so I thought. The representative never forced me to try the chair but simply pointed out its advantages. By the time she left, I'd been fitted for a power wheelchair.

It was soon clear the wheelchair was no luxury but a necessity. Each time I had a flareup of my MS, my body was left weaker than before. Physical therapy helped build up weakened muscles, but they never strengthened to my previous level. A major turning point came when my doctors and physical therapists insisted on my obtaining a service dog. A dog meant I needed help. Which I didn't.

Or so I thought. As a wife, mother, and teacher, I'd done my best to meet the needs of my husband, children, and students. MS was now infringing on my ability to fulfill my self-proclaimed duties. But with a few adaptations I could still manage, I kept telling myself.

Unfortunately, it seemed my caregivers knew more about me than I realized. Public doors began to stand sentry, keeping me from going inside. Steps might as well have been walls, making sure I didn't get past. I finally admitted I needed more assistance. Maybe a service dog *could* help.

Then again, if God really cared about me, wouldn't he make it possible for me to do everything I'd done in the past? I'd been a committed Christian for most of my life. My family and I attended church regularly. In fact, the school where my husband and I taught was a Christian school. My faith in God's love and care for me had always been strong.

But now I was finding that faith wavering. Did God really care for me? If so, why would he let my health continue to spiral downward? After all, he knew I had a family to care for and students who needed me. Accepting my need for a wheelchair had been bad enough. A service dog would be yet another visible sign I was sick. People would view me as a liability to society rather than an asset.

Each exacerbation of my MS weakened my body, signaling I should listen to the professionals and get a service dog. But when I finally acquiesced to their prodding, I learned that the waiting time would be six to eighteen months. Once again, I questioned myself as to my need, and I questioned God as to what he was doing with my life.

Then I got a call. Much earlier than anticipated, a dog had become available. I won't tell you the rest of that story here. I don't want to spoil your fun in reading later chapters. But it wasn't long before I could no longer imagine life without my canine partner. Seeing how much she loved and cared for me, I could not help but love her back. The longer we were together, the stronger our bond grew.

I began to view our bond as an analogy of the bond God wants me to enjoy with him. Previously, I couldn't comprehend how or why God would want a love relationship with me. He is God. He doesn't need me. Why would he want me to love him?

Through my loving canine companion, God has given me a glimpse of his desire for me to truly love and be loved by him. My dog doesn't need me to fulfill her doggy emotional needs, but she chooses to love me unconditionally and help me.

Maybe you have a view of God like mine was. I'd been taught that God loves and cares for me, but it was only head knowledge. My service dog has become an illustration to me that God's love is real and personal. No matter where I go or what I do, she is with me. All I have to do is turn on my power wheelchair, and she will immediately wake from a deep sleep, rise to her feet, and be ready to help me.

Not only that but our bond has restored my faith. I've come to understand that God isn't some vague entity sitting in the heavens, watching every move we make, just waiting for us to make a mess of things. He is an all-powerful heavenly Father who truly cares when we hurt and who rejoices with us at our successes. He loves you and me in a personal way and wants to have a relationship with us.

My hope as you enjoy the quirky, sometimes hilarious, sometimes challenging, but never dull adventures of my daily life with my canine partner is that you will also catch a glimpse of a loving God who wants to be there for you far more than my delightful companion does for me. May you walk away from these pages with renewed faith and a deeper relationship with the heavenly Father who loves and cares for you more than you could ever imagine.

A Matter of Faith

Chapter One
High Heels to Flats

*M*rs. Patterson, are you okay?"

"Do you need help, Mrs. Patterson?"

"Mrs. Patterson, what happened?"

It was no wonder students bombarded me with questions as I stumbled down the school hall. I looked more like a prisoner dragging a ball and chain than the teacher they'd seen just the day before. Students raced past me on their way to their next class. Meanwhile, my left shoe kept catching on the edges of the floor tiles, slowing me down. Each class began with an explanation for why I was sitting to teach.

"Many of you may have noticed my left foot dragging as I walked. Well, my shoes are old and scuffed. Dragging my foot along to wear a hole in the sole felt like a good way to get a new pair of shoes. No, actually, I have a disease called multiple sclerosis. MS for short. Up until today, it only affected the left side of my face and my left arm. But this morning I almost fell when I got up because my left foot wouldn't lift when I took a step."

By the end of the school day, dragging my left foot around had left me so tired I just wanted to go home. Instead, my husband Chas and I paid a visit to our doctor. To that point, I'd still been hoping the doctor's earlier diagnosis of multiple sclerosis was a mistake. After all, being tired all the time was normal enough for a working mom raising two children, teaching fulltime, and helping my husband, who not only taught Monday through Friday during the school year but held a second job on weekends as a certified nursing assistant (CNA) at a local nursing home. Which in turn meant that most of the childcare and housework on weekends fell to me. So maybe there really wasn't anything wrong with me.

But as I dragged my left foot into the doctor's office, I could no longer evade reality. I definitely had MS. The question was, did I have faith to handle the future?

The doctor's visit didn't turn out the way I wanted. He told me firmly, "I'm prescribing a brace for your lower left leg. It will hold your foot up to make it easier for you to walk."

"How big will it be?" I asked.

"Well, there will be a hard plastic brace running from behind your knee down the back of your leg and under your foot, stopping right before your toes."

"Will I still be able to bend my ankle?" I was trying to picture sliding this new device into the colorful, feminine high-heeled shoes I loved to wear for any dress-up occasion.

"No," the doctor responded flatly. "The brace doesn't have a hinge at the ankle."

"But if my ankle can't bend, how am I supposed to wear my dress shoes?"

"You won't."

I was not happy. Neither was I resigned. *I can't give up my pretty shoes. Pretty shoes express my femininity. I'll think of something!*

But even before my new leg brace arrived, my determination to continue expressing my femininity was put to the test. One of the classes I taught at our Christian high school was an introductory business course. My students and I worked long hours putting together the first annual business fair sponsored by our school. They contacted each of the participating vendors to become familiar with their business and observe in real life the principles they'd learned in the classroom.

Part of the class grade involved displaying professional behavior and dress the night of the fair. This meant I had to set a positive example by dressing professionally and interacting adeptly with the vendors. My students needed to see a good role model.

The school gymnasium where the business fair took place stood as a faded, aged relic from bygone years. Since there were no windows, the cinderblock walls had been painted light-green in an attempt to brighten the atmosphere. The markings of a basketball court adorned the concrete floor. At each end stood a regulation hoop with glass backboard. The only illumination came from large fluorescent lights that looked like upside-down flower canisters.

Excitement filled the air. The vendors had put a lot of effort into making their displays look extra-special. Many of them had never before participated in a business fair. Plus this one fit their marketing budget—free!

A few minutes before the fair was due to open to the public, I went into a back room and donned a pair of high-heeled shoes. They were an attractive cream with taupe-colored toes. They were also quite comfortable, just two-inch heels and simple cut around the foot. Unfortunately, I quickly discovered even that was too much for my uncooperative left foot.

I've got to do it! I told myself firmly. *There is no way I can back out now. I must set a good example that a woman can be feminine and still compete in the business world. But this is sure going to be a long night. I can barely stand, let alone walk in these!*

Opening the door into the gym, I scanned the room to find the nearest table I could grab onto so I wouldn't fall. I worked my way from table to table, keeping one hand on the tabletop to brace myself. So much for making a good impression. Dragging one lifeless foot while staggering along in heels looked more like a clown attempting to walk on stilts for the first time than a professional career woman.

Noticing my awkward gait, my husband Chas suggested I change shoes into the flat, comfortable ones I wore in the classroom.

"I can't. My school shoes don't go with this outfit. Besides, they're old and scuffed from being dragged all day. Definitely not very professional-looking."

"You don't look very professional anyway holding onto each table like that," Chas told me bluntly. "You have to take those off before you fall and break a bone."

"I'll be okay!" I insisted.

"No, you won't. Go change your shoes."

As much as I didn't want to admit it, I knew my husband was right. Turning around, I headed for the back room with a fake smile on my face. I wasn't going to allow anyone to see the hurt I was feeling. Entering the room, I snatched up the shoe box in which I'd brought my change of high heels to the school. It still held the original tissue paper in which this beautiful pair of shoes had been wrapped when I bought them to protect them from the scratches of life.

Lifting the lid, I took off one shoe and wrapped it in its tissue paper, then gently settled it into the box. *One sign of my femininity laid to rest!*

As I removed my other shoe and wrapped it up, tears dampened the tissue paper. When I reluctantly tucked the shoe into its resting place, it felt as though my womanliness had just died. My very image of myself now lay buried with those beautiful high heels in the casket of a cardboard box. Clutching my treasure to my chest, I silently wept at the death of who I'd been—an attractive, feminine, vivacious woman.

People won't look at me as they did before. They'll see me as a cripple unable to do things for myself and needing pity. I don't want pity!

Before I went to bed that night, I lovingly placed my entire collection of pretty, feminine dress shoes in the back of my closet. *If*

I end up in a wheelchair someday unable to walk, I comforted myself, *at least I'll be able pull them all back out and wear them again.*

From then on, my new normal included a brace from my left knee to my toes. Footwear had to fit over the brace while also accommodating my right foot that had no brace. Finding shoes to fit both sizes proved almost impossible unless I wanted clunky old-fashioned industrial footwear. Forget pretty or feminine!

How will I ever feel like a woman again? I'm not sure I have enough faith to face this trial.

Little did I know what God had in store for me. I never dreamed he would one day use a four-legged companion to mature my faith.

Chapter Two
Getting Faith

As the days and weeks, then months and years went on, each MS attack left more battle scars. Now my weak legs necessitated sitting and using an overhead projector to teach. Outside the classroom, I had succumbed to using a three-wheeled scooter. At first this was just for going from the house or school to the car. But eventually I needed it to get around the school corridors and sometimes even around the house.

"You sure are a good driver with that thing," fellow teachers and students alike would remark.

"You should see all the nicks and dings on the furniture and doorframes in my house," I replied. "I practice there so I don't ruin someone else's property."

Doctors prescribed physical therapy to increase my body strength, but it couldn't heal my fears. Would I ever be able to walk again? Would I even be able to write on the overhead projector to teach? This was all new territory, and I wanted answers. There were none. No prescription could be written to guarantee a return to full function of my weak body.

"I would say welcome back," my therapist remarked as I entered the large gym-like room for the first time after a period of remission. "But since you're here for physical therapy, that means you've had an exacerbation of your MS. We'll see what we can do to strengthen your muscles again."

Treadmills, parallel bars, and raised mats gave the room an air of normalcy as though this was just a visit to the gym. But that illusion faded when I glanced at the far wall where wheelchairs, walkers, and other adaptive equipment sat in straight rows as if waiting for inspection. One particular arm exercise proved difficult for me as well as my therapist. What looked like half of a hula-hoop stood on a table. On one side of the arc were stacked little pieces of plastic. My assigned task was to lift each piece up and over the arch to the other side without dropping it at the top.

The object of this exercise was to strengthen my left arm so I could write on the blackboard. But it took a number of sessions before I got a single piece of plastic over the top. Even then, I wasn't allowed to let go of the piece so it would slide the rest of the way on its own. I had to set it down on the far side. If I worked my arm too hard, it would rebel by flying around, making me look like someone swatting at a swarm of bees. The therapist found it difficult to catch my arm and maintain it in the only position that would stop the flailing.

Leg exercises to strengthen weak muscles exhausted any remaining energy I had. The more I concentrated on getting my legs strong enough to walk again, the more the need for assistance became apparent. But I didn't want to give up. By now I had also progressed from the scooter to a power wheelchair, which to me felt as though I was giving in to my disease.

Please God, I need to walk! I prayed. *Is my faith so weak that it is keeping me from getting better? I have to keep working at this if for no other reason than to prove to myself I can.*

"Your progress has slowed," my physical therapist finally announced at the end of a session. "It looks like your body has reached a plateau. Insurance will no longer pay for any more sessions."

But I'm not ready to stop! I cried out silently. *I need to keep trying. The weaker I get, the more people will look at me like an invalid and pity me. I don't want pity. All I need is a little help.*

The therapist was still speaking. "With the weakness in your arms, you might want to consider a service animal to help you."

I had no idea what she was talking about. "What is a service animal?"

"Well, a service animal goes everywhere with you to help accomplish tasks you have trouble performing."

"Like what?"

"They can pick up things off the floor and give them to you. You mentioned you have a hard time opening doors. They could open them for you. There are many other things they are trained to do."

My curiosity was piqued. "What kind of animal are we talking about?"

"Well, dogs are most common."

"A dog is no go," I told the therapist firmly. "My husband is allergic to them. Besides, I don't consider myself so disabled I need that kind of help."

End of discussion. At least for a few years until an exacerbation of my MS left me completely immobile. My limbs laughed at me when asked to move. Breathing took effort to the point that I found myself flat on my back in the hospital.

To alleviate my anxiety, the hospital assigned a certified nursing assistant (CNA) named Sheri to sit with me the first night. During my hospital stay, Sheri and I became good friends. Sometime after I returned home, she had to vacate her apartment, so Chas and I invited her to move into our upstairs. Having her vibrant personality and practical help around the house seemed a much better option than a service dog. Besides, she didn't bark, and my husband wasn't allergic to her.

Life took on a comfortable routine. God had answered my prayers. The case for a service dog was closed. Or so I thought until three years later when Chas came home from his annual allergy checkup and announced, "Guess what! I'm no longer allergic to dogs. All those years of shots finally paid off."

"Yay!" I cheered. "Can we get a pet dog now? A cuddly lap dog like I had growing up? Please!"

"No. Dogs stay outside, period," was his response.

Well, if dogs had to stay outside, Chas wouldn't be open to a service dog either. So much for the dog idea. Again, I put the possibility from my mind.

Then I began noticing service dog information showing up in magazines. When our local newspaper advertised a service dog demonstration, I began wondering if God was telling me something. The night of the demonstration, I convinced Chas to go with me. It wouldn't hurt to glean some information.

As I waited for the demonstration to begin, I strolled in my wheelchair through the aisles of exhibits. In one of the booths, I noticed a woman in a motorized wheelchair like mine. Asleep beside her was what looked like a dog with a saddle on its back. How could it sleep with all these people around and so much noise?

"Hi, my name is Joan," I introduced myself to the woman. "You sure do have an amazing dog there."

"My name is Lori, and his name is Fennec."

"Amazing. What all does he do for you?"

"He opens and closes doors, picks up things I drop, gets the phone, pays the cashier, and carries things for me. Those are just a few of the things he does."

"It's hard to believe a dog can do all those things. I have MS and wear out quickly."

"So do I. He helps save my energy."

Our conversation included Fennec demonstrating his skills. This amazing dog picked objects off the floor and handed them to her. He gently took her jacket sleeve in his mouth and pulled it off.

That very evening with encouragement from Chas, I downloaded the application and filled it out. The next morning, I dropped it into the mail. Was God really leading me? Was I jumping to conclusions? The faith that had dwindled down into a few small embers in the depths of my heart began flickering to life again. Did I dare fan the flame?

A few weeks later, *Canine Partners for Life* called to set up an interview. Was this a sign? What if they didn't think I was disabled enough to need a dog? Could I even get through the process of getting a dog?

The days between the call and the interview seemed to drag. One day I felt confident this was what I should do. The next, doubt ruled my thoughts. My faith was as up and down as a rollercoaster.

Interview day finally arrived sunny and hot. My air-conditioned van should have made my trip pleasant and cool. It didn't. My body sat rigid behind a steering wheel slick with sweat where I held it in a death grip.

As I turned into the entrance to the *Canine Partners for Life* premises, large, green fields surrounded on three sides with buildings welcomed me. Out to one side, I could see a concrete edifice with a fenced-in area. Straight ahead was a large, blue aluminum building. On the left was a relatively small ranch house. That would be the office according to the instructions I'd been given.

A pleasant woman greeted me as I entered the ranch house, directing me to a waiting room where a large picture window faced a sprawling green lawn. The walls were adorned with dog pictures and plaques listing donor names. Tastefully arranged shelves held information brochures. On one, I saw a little stuffed dog dressed in a blue rain cape.

Engrossed in my new surroundings, I was startled when two women entered, each with a dog at their side. They escorted me into a conference room with a large table. As I positioned my wheelchair at the table, they introduced themselves as the two trainers, Megan and Deb. Their dogs settled obediently under the table. They were in their last phase of training, I was told.

The interview began with a short explanation about the training and matching process. The dogs spend their first year in a puppy home. There they learn basic skills like potty-training and not eating shoes. Sometime after their first birthday, the dogs return to the *Canine Partners for Life* kennel for more in-depth training. The next year is spent teaching them general skills such as opening and closing doors or picking up objects and giving them to the trainer. I was amazed at the depth of training they received.

At that point, the interview turned into an interrogation. Or at least it felt so to me.

"What do you like to do in your free time?" one trainer asked.

What does that have to do with a dog? I wasn't expecting questions like this. How do I answer it? Will they think I don't deserve a dog?

As the questions raced through my mind, I tried to formulate an acceptable answer. "Well, I used to crochet and then cross-stitch. Now I read a lot."

"Which hand do you use most?" the other trainer put in.

Now I know either I'm crazy or they are! Why in the world would they need to know that? But I answered calmly, "I am left-handed, but my left arm is my weakest limb. So I guess I use my right hand the most these days."

"Have you ever had a dog before?"

"Yes. Growing up, we had a little Chihuahua/fox terrier mix. He was almost sixteen when he died. Chas and I had a beagle for a while after we were married. I love dogs, but I've never had a large one."

I relaxed, and answers flowed more easily. The interview finally ended, and Megan began my tour of the grounds. The large blue aluminum building was the training barn. The inside was a single wide-open space with a concrete floor where the dogs did some of their training. The next building was the one with the fenced-in area. As the door opened, we were greeted with dog sounds reminding their keepers not to forget dinnertime.

To our right was a small room with a picture window. It was a snuggle room, I learned, where volunteers came to hold, pet, and nurture the new puppies. *What a great idea!* There were cats wandering the halls. Two cages, one occupied with a rabbit and one with a guinea pig, stood against the walls.

"Why all these different animals?" I asked.

"We introduce the dogs to them," Megan answered, "so they get used to being around other animals and not reacting to them. After all, they might end up placed in a home where other animals are already living."

She escorted me into a larger, brightly-lit room with stacks of dog food in one corner and a large stainless-steel sink in another. A volunteer was standing at a large cart that held food dishes waiting to be filled with the evening meal. She was engrossed in looking at a list as she worked.

"I guess feeding all these dogs is quite a job," I commented.

"Yes. Some dogs have special feeding instructions. That is why she refers to her list," Megan said.

They sure take good care of their dogs! Excitement was beginning to build in me. Getting a dog might be a better idea than I'd originally thought. God definitely had his hand on the direction I was to go. By the time the tour was finished, I was ready and eager to get my dog.

But the trainer's parting comment erased all my excitement. "If you are found eligible for the program, the wait time to receive a dog is six to eighteen months."

I felt immediately deflated. "Wow! I didn't realize it was so involved."

We exchanged parting niceties. Megan turned around and began walking across the open field toward the house. Heading back to my van, I began a conversation with God. *Just a minute! I finally muster enough faith to apply for a dog, and now you tell me I have to wait? This wasn't in the plan. You showed me what to do. So why aren't you doing it?*

This was not my way of doing things. Once I understand the idea of what to do, I charge ahead full force, knocking over anyone in my way. Was God playing a game with me? If so, it wasn't funny at all. God was to open doors. In my mind, eighteen months was a very long time to be waiting. My health could deteriorate significantly by then.

Each day, service dog thoughts battled for position in my mind. One day my faith was strong, resting in God's timing. The next, I would fight to keep from accusing God for the long wait time. God was teaching me to have faith in his timing.

Then one day the phone rang. "Hello. This is Susanne Guy from *Canine Partners for Life.* Is Joan Patterson there?"

"This is Joan." My heart raced, and my blood pressure rose. *Did something happen to disqualify me from the program before I even get started?*

"The trainers asked me to call you. Unexpectedly, we have a dog available that might work for you. Would you be interested?"

"Yes, I would be." *Are you kidding? Absolutely, I'm interested!*

"Great. We would like to set up a time for you to come and meet the dog. Could we schedule a date now?"

"Absolutely."

We set a date to meet my "answer to prayer." One short phone conversation, and my faith was back on track.

Sheri came with me for support. Once again, my van's steering wheel was coated with perspiration from my hands. Prayers asking God to show me his will filled the drive time. I didn't want to make a mistake. As we entered the grounds, I sent up one last prayer. *God, please make it clear if this is the dog you want for me.*

We were ushered into the same waiting room as before. This time, I was sure everyone around me could hear my heart pounding in my chest. Time stopped.

Megan entered the room with a beautiful black Labrador retriever by her side. Its full attention on her, the dog sat when she sat. A sleek, midnight-black ball of controlled energy now faced me, its deep-brown eyes focused on mine, full of anticipation. I fell immediately in love.

Megan's next words will be forever etched in my memory. "This is the dog we have in mind for you. Her name is Faith."

Her name is Faith? Faith! God, you used all but neon lights to show me your will.

Many years have passed since God introduced Faith into my life. Opening doors? Easy. Picking up dropped objects? No problem. Walking through a store proudly carrying an Auntie Anne's soft pretzel bag in her mouth and hearing astonished comments? Priceless.

Every time I say her name, it serves as a reminder God does reveal his will. It's just A MATTER OF FAITH!

Chapter Three
Change of Loyalty

*E*xcitement and apprehension coursed through me as I packed my luggage into the van. The jet-black dog with dark-brown eyes and lashes—the one who had stolen my heart the first time we met—would be coming home with me in just three weeks. Mandatory supplies for Faith were carefully tucked into the back of my van, ready to be ferried to the *Canine Partners for Life* facility where Faith and I would be undergoing our training together.

Three weeks? It seems a long time for learning to work with a dog.

The list of items I'd been instructed to purchase and bring with me was a long one. Food was logical, but so much? I decided to take just a portion of the twenty-five-pound bag with me. A brush to keep her coat shiny.

Faith also needed toys to play with after a long day of working, but I needed to be careful about what kind. Labrador retrievers have strong mouths, which they like to use to destroy unsuspecting playthings in minutes. Kong brand had been recommended because they were the most indestructible. But this particular brand contained latex, a substance to which I had a severe allergy, so their products were off-limits. It made finding suitable things for her difficult.

I spent the first night in my hotel room organizing my things and preparing for Faith. The more I looked at all the things for her, the more nervous I got. This was going to be a huge change in my life, and now reality set in. Sleep came and went. I looked at the alarm clock multiple times. I couldn't be late the first day because of oversleeping.

Dressed, breakfast finished, supplies for the first day packed, I headed from the hotel the next morning to the *Canine Partners for Life* facility, excitement and fear all wrapped together. There were twelve human-canine pairs in my class. As Faith and I waited to begin our three-week team training, I had no idea what was going to happen. The very thought of taking control of such a big dog intimidated me. Looking around at the crowd of people and dogs, I began to get cold feet about proceeding.

I am going to embarrass myself. Will this beautiful dog they've worked so hard to train even want to be with me after she sees how stupid I am? What in the world have I gotten myself into?

Our first lesson was learning how to dress our dogs with the necessary equipment. The first item looked like a miniature horse saddle. Mine had a tall metal U-shaped handle protruding from its middle into the air for me to hold onto when I walked.

Three straps and clasps. Looks easy enough.

We were then each handed a harness specific to our dog. My classmates shared my ignorance as we tried to follow the trainer's instructions. What looked so easy as she demonstrated how to dress a dog somehow turned into a jigsaw puzzle when I began fumbling with the straps and latches. Faith stood patiently while I tried to slide a head halter over her nose and fasten it around her neck. This would help me guide her when we moved around. I was holding the halter, trying to decide how to put it on, when Faith inserted her nose through the opening. She knew what to do.

Getting the equipment onto Faith turned out to be the easy part. Three trainers, Deb Bauer, Megan Esherick, and Roberta Knauf, along with director Darlene Sullivan with her own service dog, labored session after session to teach us what was already second nature to our dogs. This included learning a completely new vocabulary. Faith had grown up versed in "service dogease." She knew exactly what and how to meet my needs if I could only remember the right vocabulary to tell her to lie down or other commands.

We're only beginning, and I'm already lost. It's going to be a long three weeks!

Part of selecting a particular dog was based on the disabled person's needs as well as to match their personalities. Faith was social like me, which proved difficult in public. She wanted to get to know people around her rather than stay focused on me.

Thankfully, her eagerness to please helped both of us. She would wait patiently while I struggled to find the correct word for the task. She often ended up doing what I wanted before I could even tell her. She would see the other dogs doing something and just copy them.

Once Faith's equipment was in place, we moved on to taking our place in a line with the other human-canine teams, ready to begin walking around the perimeter of the room. Because I'm left-handed, "starting position" for me meant Faith sat by my right side while everyone else's dog sat on their left. Now I understood why the trainer had asked me in the interview which hand I used most.

We were then instructed to give our dogs the command to begin walking. I searched my computer brain for the correct file and got an error message. While I was processing, Faith took her cue from the others and began walking, once again on my right while the other dogs walked on the left.

Good dog. She is so smart. I can't believe how much she loves me already. My heart swelled with pride and admiration for my new partner. We were becoming a team. I knew we were destined for each other.

Then the trainers brought me back to reality. They warned our class not to get too complacent about our dog's eagerness. They were currently enjoying showing off all they knew. But at some point during training, each dog would decide they'd had enough and suddenly refuse to do anything their new partner asked. This was what the trainers called a meltdown. It was a natural occurrence as the dog transferred its loyalty from the trainer to its new partner. There was no question whether it would happen. But when, where, and how long depended on the dog.

The reason this occurred was because only one trainer had worked with each dog during the past year, sharpening the skills it would need. Our dogs had bonded with their trainers. During the transfer process, this special person who had nurtured each dog and worked with them would not look at or so much as acknowledge the dog. Demonstrating tricks for a new partner was fun at first. Then the dog would decide enough was enough. It wanted its own trainer back. Like toddlers demanding their mommy, the dogs would stop working until they got their own way. Or so they thought.

Faith's loyalty is already apparent, I told myself. *She clearly loves me. If she's having this expected meltdown, her rebellion must have been such a small one I didn't even notice.*

One day, teams were scattered around the large concrete-floored building, practicing individual tasks. I was to have Faith pick up an item from the floor and place it in a white plastic wash basket sitting in the middle of what looked like a conglomeration of adult toys—hairbrush, leather gardening glove, small metal cooking pot, scrub brush, and other sundry items.

I'll get her to pick up the leather glove, I decided. *She's done this numerous times. Easy. I even remember the command for it. Then we can move on to something else.*

I approached the glove with confidence. "Faith, take it."

She stood still as if she didn't hear me.

"Faith, take it," I repeated, my confidence crumbling.

She once again refused to obey my command.

Darlene, the director, approached with her service dog by her side. "Congratulations. Faith has decided to melt down."

"So, what do I do now?" I asked, hoping my voice didn't betray my fear of working through it.

"Don't give in. Keep giving her the command until she realizes she isn't going to get her way." Darlene was emphatic and non-sympathetic. "If you give in, she has won, and you will never get her loyalty."

"How long will that take?"

"Till she's good and ready to listen to you. It could be a few minutes or a few days. It's up to her."

"What if she doesn't take it at all?"

"We will cross that bridge if we need to." Darlene gave me an encouraging smile as she moved along to help another team.

Great! God, please don't have it be long. I'm exhausted, and I'm not up for a battle of wills. Are you trying to tell me something, God?

Frustrated, I continued. "Faith, take it."

No response as Faith stood in front of me, not moving a muscle. It was if she'd suddenly become totally deaf.

"Faith, I said take it."

Still no response. I might as well have been talking to a statue.

"Take." Pause. "It!"

My voice was rising and my doggy infatuation dying. The stalemate continued with neither side backing down. Not giving in was easier said than followed. I entertained the idea of moving to another object, hoping she'd be willing to pick up something different.

"Take . . . It!"

My pleading turned to begging, then begging evolved into anger as we played this new Take It game. Finally, utter desperation overtook my anger. My vision blurred as tears filled my eyes. They were just about to cascade down my cheeks when Faith picked up the leather glove and gave it to me.

"You did it! You did it!" My spontaneous joyful shouts reverberated through the training barn.

Faith did a happy dance while I jumped up and down in my wheelchair. From then on, Faith and I worked together as a team, becoming one as we learned each other's needs and how to meet them.

But that initial struggle between Faith and me reminds me how we battle God for our own way. Through our stubborn will, we ignore his calling. But our loving heavenly Father patiently waits, never giving up on us until we are ready to focus our lives on him.

No wonder heavenly angels sing when a sinner commits his life to God.

At least the war was over, and Faith's loyalty had been firmly transferred to me as her new partner. While I wasn't sure Faith and I would ever be as precise in task execution as soldiers marching in formation, we now had a lifetime to work on it.

Or so I thought. While I may have won this battle, my assumption the war was over proved erroneous. Faith may have conceded I was her new partner, but that didn't mean there were no more hurdles to cross.

Chapter Four
Baby Steps

"Congratulations!" Darlene Sullivan, founder of *Canine Partner for Life*, told our class the very first day of the three-week course. "You've just made the commitment to be married to a two-year-old for the rest of your life."

Oh no! I found myself reacting. I hadn't thought that far ahead. *The rest of my life? I'm just trying to get through each day. And a two-year-old? It's been a long time since I worked with a two-year-old. I'm not ready for this after all. What does she mean? If I have to think and act like a two-year-old, I can't do it.*

For Darlene and the three trainers, turning a group of twelve novices into responsible dog handlers was a daunting task. Our canine partners knew a language foreign to us. I soon felt like a two-year-old trying to learn vocabulary words so Faith would do what I wanted.

This included certain words for the different positions Faith could assume while I was standing still. Front and back were logical. Heel and side were new words to me. I'd heard the term heel but didn't realize it meant a certain place. Heel meant Faith was to be on my left. Side meant she was to be on my right.

Harder to remember was that heel is the normal default terminology for a dog taking their position at their partner's side (excuse the pun, please). Since I'm left-handed, the trainers had to work with Faith once we were matched so she would walk and work on my right side instead of my left.

Early in the training, I learned to watch and listen to classmates who were training with a successor dog rather than their first service dog. They already knew what to do and what words to use. Observing them worked until it came to positioning our dogs. Everyone else told their dogs to "heel." I had to remember to use the command "side" so Faith would take her position to my right instead of my left.

Aaaaahhh! I'm never going to get this right. How long does it take to get the knack of this? If Faith is the two-year-old, I'm not even two!

The harder I worked, the more stressed I got. I felt like a failure. I was becoming certain Faith and I would never pass the certification test at the end of training. Nothing seemed to stick in my rememberer, and my forgetterer was working overtime.

Each day's training began with our teams in a line, our canine partners sitting at the proper place beside us.

"Begin walking to your right," one trainer would instruct.

We were all to say, "Forward." Our dogs would then stand up and begin walking by our side in a circle around the training area.

"Now turn around away from your dogs and go the opposite direction," the trainer instructed next.

Away from our dogs? Aye! I turn one way while everyone else turns the other. I am always so different.

It took me a little while to figure out what the trainer meant. By the time I processed her directive and headed in the opposite direction, teams behind me were waiting. *I am so slow!*

"Those with black dogs keep walking. The rest stand still."

Since Faith was among the black dogs, we now had to weave around other teams while keeping our dogs on task. It was hard enough keeping in my mind what I was to be doing while also keeping Faith from socializing with the other dogs as we passed them. She was so distractible. One trainer had mentioned to me before we started that Faith was quite the social dog. I hadn't understood what she meant at the time. I certainly did after a few passes.

"Those with black dogs stand still while the rest of you begin walking."

Ahh! A breather. No, Faith! You aren't supposed to visit with the dogs walking by.

"Those still walking turn around towards your dog and go in the opposite direction."

That's nice. At least now I can see them coming.

"Those standing still begin walking the direction you are facing."

Great! Now I have to keep her with me and not wandering off to say hi to her friends as we pass by. My head is swimming.

New words. New skills. New information. My brain was in overload. By the end of the day, my brain was mush from thinking so hard. The bed was so inviting when I got back to the hotel. Turning off my brain, I fell into bed, oblivious to what lay ahead.

Each day, we began our workout by standing in a line and then walking around the training barn in a circle. Faith and I were getting better at knowing what to do when instructed, or so I thought.

"Today you will learn how to use your voice so your dog will obey," said the trainer.

I thought we were doing that already.

"I want you to have your dog sit in front of you. Then I want you to say the names of vegetables while looking at your dog and using a stern voice."

Is she crazy?

"Faith, front. Sit. Carrots. Celery. Corn. Sweet potatoes. Beans. Tomatoes." *Help. I'm running out of vegetable names.*

"Did you notice how your dog reacted? Your dog will not necessarily know what the words are but how you say the words. Now I want you to tell your dog it is naughty. Use scolding words but in a voice reflecting praise."

Now I know she has lost her mind!

Looking at Faith with a broad smile, I began a diatribe of insults in a lighthearted voice. "Faith, you are the dumbest dog. Yes, you are. You don't do a thing I ask you. You don't listen to me when I give you a command."

Okay, I'm beginning to understand what she's saying. What it is she wants us to learn. This is actually starting to make sense.

"You will use three voices with your dog," the trainer went on. "When you want it to do something, issue a command. Your voice should be serious to make clear you mean what you say. If your dog needs correction, you must use an authoritative voice so they know they've done something wrong. Last but not least, you need to praise your dog frequently. To let your dog know you are pleased, use a happy voice. Some of your so-called stern voices just now sounded like you were giving an invitation to a tea party."

Her explanation led me to think of how God speaks to us. We can't see his face or audibly hear his voice, but we do sense his presence. When we do something pleasing to him, we feel his pleasure in our conscience. Likewise, we know when we have done something wrong. He shows his displeasure through our conscience.

We'd been instructed to bring small dog treats each day to use for teaching. These little morsels along with a clicker would become our closest allies. The clicker was simply a device that looked like a finger-sized remote and made a clicking sound each time you pushed the button. Each time our dogs accomplished the given command, we were to make a single click and give them a corresponding treat.

Learning to give commands to our dogs was a new experience for most of us. I was used to doing things like taking my coat off without thinking. Now I not only had to think consciously about what I wanted Faith to do but to breakdown the simplest task into steps. Each step had to be completed before moving on to the next one.

"You will learn how to have your dog take something from you, hold onto it, then give it back to you," said one of the trainers.

That can't be hard!

"When you want your dog to do something, you say their name first, then the command. Tell you dog to 'take it.' Once they take the object from you, say, 'give it.' Your dog should then place the object in your hand. Remember, say your dog's name first, then the command."

How am I going to remember all that?

"And once your dog returns the object to you, don't forget to click and treat."

I held out the object we were using for practice. "Faith, take it."

She took it from me like a pro, eyes fixed on my face as she awaited my next command. *She is so attentive!*

"Faith, give."

She placed the object back in my hands. I tried to remember to click the moment she released it. My frustration rose from the effort of trying to click and treat at the same time. Faith knew what she was supposed to do, but I had such a hard time trying to remember all the steps, especially clicking the clicker and giving the treat all at the same time.

"I can't seem to get this right," I complained to the trainer. "She does it before I have a chance to click. I don't have enough arms. I need one arm to take the object from her, another one to click, and another to treat. I'm just not fast enough."

"Joan, you don't have to give a treat right way," the trainer assured me. "Just take it from her and click. The important part is to click as soon as she does what you want her to do. Then you can take your time to give her the treat."

"Oh, wow! That helps so much. I'm just not that fast to do all of it at once."

"You're not supposed to be."

Once I started clicking as soon as Faith did what I asked, she caught on faster to what I wanted.

And that too makes me think of how God works with his children. He doesn't expect us to understand everything all at once. He uses our small experiences as baby steps to teach us basic skills, reassuring us along the way. Then he builds onto what we've learned to accomplish more. He patiently takes his time with us, never giving us a new task to perform that he hasn't first prepared us to do for him.

Chapter Five
Paying the Cashier

"Oh, look. How cute!"

"Look at that dog carrying a package."

The more comments Faith heard, the higher she held her head, package dangling from her mouth. She was so proud to carry any package through a store, no matter how far, and thoroughly enjoyed the attention this drew. Listening to people's exclamations when they saw her always made me smile.

But while this became a norm during the ten years Faith and I worked together as a team, we definitely didn't start out that way. One of the tasks we had to accomplish during training was for Faith to take my wallet in her mouth, stand on her back legs, and give it to a cashier to pay for a purchase. Faith would then return to sitting position, staring at my wallet. Whenever the cashier moved it, her eyes would follow. She looked like she was scrutinizing every movement to make sure the cashier processed my purchase correctly.

Once the cashier was finished, Faith would then reverse the process, accepting my wallet from the cashier, taking her legs off the counter, then giving the wallet to me. Once she returned my wallet, she would put her front paws back on the counter to retrieve my purchase, then carry the purchase to a designated table somewhere in the store.

During our training sessions at the *Canine Partners for Life* facility, we practiced having our dogs give something to a trainer standing behind a table. The trainers supplied the object to be given and retrieved. Faith and I practiced until we could do this without any mishaps. She began to understand my cues. I in turn began to understand how to give her the object and where to place my wheelchair so she had room to stand on her back legs and give whatever was in her mouth to the person behind the table. We were functioning together the way we were expected. Or so I thought.

For the first week, we had all been meeting up with our canine partners each morning at the facility. At the end of the day, they would return to their kennels while we returned to our hotel rooms. The first Friday, we joined our dogs in the morning, but that evening we took them back with us to the hotel. From that point on, Faith was at my side just as she would be once I took her home.

By now, our field trips incorporated more advanced tasks. With each field trip, I grew more confident with Faith. She performed each task the trainers gave us. I began to relax out in public with my partner by my side. At least until our all-day trip to Longwood Gardens, a world-famous horticulturalist's dream.

Our group gathered outside the front door into the estate near a large concrete urn that held a precisely trimmed tree reaching for the sky. I was so excited to be visiting such a renowned place. Huge manicured lawns, multiple gardens each with its own theme, and greenhouses with all kinds of exotic plants awaited us. It would be a relaxing break from the pressures of dog basic training.

My preconceived enjoyment burst when a trainer explained the purpose for coming to this particular location. "You have learned many skills with your dog. Today you will have ample opportunity to practice being a team. We will be going to different areas of the gardens. The trainers will have various items awaiting you. Do what is asked. When everyone is finished, the group will move to the next station to practice something different."

How many things do they have for us?

"You have been practicing 'go pay' with your dogs. Today you will use that skill to pay for your admission. When we get to the cashier, form a line. Each person will get the opportunity to have your dog pay. Don't worry about the cashier. They are very understanding and are used to our group needing some extra time."

My hands got sweaty the closer we got to the cashier. I had mixed expectations. Faith had flawlessly executed the task of paying for things in practice. The last time we'd practiced, she'd been so excited to give the object to the trainer, I'd thought she was going to jump on top of the table. She'd also eagerly retrieved what the trainer had in her hand. This time she'd be using my actual wallet, not a prop from the trainers.

I watched the other dogs in our class giving their partner's wallet to the cashier. Some had no trouble, performing like pros. Some classmates had difficulty getting their dog to take the wallet or having them give it to the cashier.

Please God, let Faith do this for me. She did it so easily in practice.

"Joan, you're next," the trainer told me.

My heart raced as we approached the cashier. I held out my leather change purse, which was only large enough for a few folded bills and some coins. "Faith, take it."

She gave a perfect impression of a statue. Not a muscle moved. Her mouth stayed closed as a clam, eyes glazed over.

What's wrong! Faith, you have to do it. We're holding up the whole crowd. You're embarrassing me! Aloud, I said with my command voice, "Faith, take it."

Still no movement. And so it began. I tried turning around with Faith and coming back at the task again as if it were something new. Didn't fool her. No matter what I tried, the result was the same. Faith stood beside me, making no attempt to open her mouth to receive my leather change purse. I even tried stuffing it in her mouth but with no success.

The trainers finally suggested I use a high-powered treat, one she really liked, as a bribe. I took out one of her favorites, the ones Faith would normally do anything to get. She didn't move. I fleetingly thought she'd died and rigor mortis had set in.

My emotions ran the gamut from anger to pleading to rage to begging, all while trying to keep some outward appearance of calmness. No matter how I tried to reason with her, Faith was determined not to take my change purse.

I looked at a trainer. "I'm holding up the line. Why don't I let someone else go. Faith and I can go to the end of the line and try again after everyone else is finished."

"No. You continue. The cashiers are used to us being here with a training class. They will open another window if they feel it is necessary."

Great! There is no way I'm going to get out of doing it.

Returning to the task at hand, I hugged Faith, crying softly into her fur and asking her to please take the change purse. I was so desperate I even tried reasoning with her. The rest of the class started rooting for us. "You can do it. You're a great team. Don't give up."

It felt like years since we'd begun our change purse stand-off. I was getting fatigued from all the physical and emotional exertion. Trainer or not, I was about to give up when Faith opened her mouth, took my change purse, stood on her back legs, and gave it to the cashier. The lady took the change purse as if it was the most natural thing to do, processed the admission, and with a smile handed the purse back to Faith.

Will she take it? Am I going to have to go through this all over again? There is no way I can do this again, especially working with someone else.

Faith took the purse like a piece of candy and returned it to me.

"You did it! You did it! I'm so proud of you. Yay!" From all the clapping and cheers, every visitor to the gardens in close proximity to us must be aware Faith had finally done what she was supposed to do. My cheeks were wet with happy tears.

We retreated to stand beside a trainer along with the other teams who'd already completed their ordeal. As another team moved up to take their turn, I commented with frustration, "I don't know why Faith was so stubborn. She has done so well in practice."

"Actually, she wasn't just being stubborn, Joan," the trainer explained kindly. "When Faith was a puppy, she ate two leather leashes. I guess her puppy raiser got through to her that leather is not for eating. She learned her lesson well to the point she now resists putting anything leather in her mouth."

I was reminded of our last stand-off with the leather glove. "Well! I wish I would have known that. I could have used something else."

"No." The trainer shook her head firmly. "She has to learn when it is appropriate and when it is not."

I'd been feeling so angry and confused about why Faith wouldn't listen to me and take my leather change purse. I now felt compassion. She'd simply been holding fast to the lesson learned long ago. I hugged her with new understanding and love.

It was a reminder that God doesn't get upset with me when he teaches me something different even when I close my mind and keep my body rigid, refusing to listen to his soft urging. His patience never falters. If only I would remain as faithful to him!

Chapter Six
Passing the Test

O h, how perspectives change! Before I started training with Faith, three weeks seemed a long time to learn how to work with a dog. In my mind, all I had to learn was how to get a dog to listen, then complete the required task.

Then reality hit. Trying to get a dog to understand what to do was like playing charades. We both knew the intended result. Getting there was the challenge.

My job was to communicate using the correct language so Faith understood what to do. No easy task for someone who had never before worked with a dog. As long as we completed the tasks the trainers gave us, I felt confident. If Faith only completed part of a task, I had no idea how to figure out what to do to motivate her.

"Tug" was the command to pull something. One exercise was to pull on a string attached to a cabinet door so as to open the door. When instructed, Faith would walk to the cabinet door, grab the dangling string in her mouth, and tug it so lightly it barely stretched out straight, much less came close to opening the cabinet door. My job was to decipher how to get her to do what I wanted using some other method. My brain worked overtime trying to find another solution, but I usually couldn't think of anything. Thankfully, there was always a trainer nearby to help. They became our security blanket.

One healthcare item was clipping our dog's nails. The trainers demonstrated the method, then told us to find a spot and do what they showed us.

Clip Faith's nails? I asked myself incredulously. *Are you kidding? You've been doing it for years, and you want us to do something dangerous where we could hurt them? Every week? I don't do my own nails weekly. I'm afraid of taking too much and making her bleed. Faith, I sure hope you are patient with me. They tell us you can feel our emotions. I hope you can't tell mine right now or you won't let me get anywhere near you!*

I guess Faith felt my fear because she wouldn't stand still. Just as I got the trimmer in place and mustered the nerve to squeeze, she would pull her paw out of my hand, and we had to start all over again. Eighteen nails later, I was exhausted, she was stressed, and very little nail was missing. It would be an arduous task once we got home, one I hadn't expected or wanted.

Two less unpleasant parts of learning our dog's hygiene was brushing their fur and teeth. I hadn't realized Labradors shed so much. Each stroke filled the brush's bristles with black fur to the point it needed cleaned out. I began wondering if Faith would be nude by the time I finished.

Brushing her teeth was a bigger challenge. Poultry-flavored dog toothpaste applied to a dog toothbrush kept Faith watching with anticipation. I was to hold her mouth open with one hand and brush with the other. No one told her what was going to occur. She allowed me to open her mouth but tried licking the toothpaste from the brush rather than allowing me to brush her teeth. I tried to move the brush back and forth to clean her teeth but wasn't making much progress. When somewhat finished, I held the brush so Faith could lick what paste remained. I felt like a failure.

So much to learn and execute correctly. Three months wouldn't be long enough, let alone only three weeks. *How am I going to do this at home? Am I up to this?*

Faith and I worked hard to perform as a team, perfecting various skills we'd need to execute together once we left our training ground and headed home. No longer would we have the security of a trainer nearby to unravel the mess we created. We'd been warned our dogs were not robots. They had a mind and personality all their own.

My early confidence morphed into inadequacy as I wrestled with my new responsibilities. Trying to remember the correct word or action so Faith would do what I wanted turned into brain fatigue. Each passing day became a stark reality of one less chance to figure out this new life the two of us were supposed to lead together. Three weeks had seemed forever, but now they raced by with still so much to learn.

At the same time, all of us in the class looked forward to graduation where we would show our family and friends our magnificent dogs. Only one event stood between us and that special moment: our final exam. Passing this certification test would allow Faith to legally accompany me anywhere in public. Together, we practiced each task multiple times to prepare for the test. This would indicate whether we could face the future as a team.

Faith did a great job practicing certain parts of the test. I was so proud of the way she got in and out of my van, trotted behind me when maneuvering tight spaces, and sauntered past scattered dog food on the floor without pausing to sniff. She saved me energy tugging off my coat, socks, and clothes. Exterior doors, once prohibitive for me, now allowed admittance when Faith and I worked together.

But there was one test task that could keep us from graduating. The one task Faith refused to complete was carrying a package after taking it from a cashier. There were so many segments to perform to get to the final objective. First, she took my wallet, stood on her back feet, placed her front feet on the counter, gave my wallet to the cashier, returned to all four feet on the ground, and sat. She then watched anxiously for the cashier to hand her back my wallet once the transaction was finished. Repeating the same process to retrieve my wallet, she then give it to me.

This part of the task was always executed with precision and gusto. The final segment required repeating the preceding process yet again to retrieve the package, then carry it to wherever I wanted. No matter how hard I worked with her, once Faith's feet touched the ground, so did the package if she perceived I wanted her to carry it somewhere. She would take an object in her mouth, hold it, and give it to me. But there was no way she was going to carry it, not even a few feet.

On one particular field trip to a farmer's market, we were to have our dogs buy something and carry it a short distance. This excursion happened to have lots of choices to practice paying for something and carrying it. In this case, Faith had to purchase and then carry a bag containing a food item to a nearby restaurant table. She excitedly gave the cashier my wallet, watching intently while the cashier opened and closed the wallet to complete the purchase. When the cashier gave her back the wallet, Faith was so thrilled she looked like she was going to jump right over the counter.

Faith handed me the wallet. Next, the cashier handed her a warm, steaming bag with a yummy soft pretzel folded inside. Once again, the package and Faith's front paws hit the floor at the same time. My heart sank along with the package. Faith knew what to do. She just didn't want to do it. I feared the pretzel would never get to its destination. No matter how often we practiced, the outcome was always the same. Grab bag. Paws down. Bag down.

Our test day arrived cool and windy. Colorful fall leaves danced through the air in celebration as other teams passed their exam. This involved driving to a location, then carrying out certain tasks, just as we'd been practicing the last three weeks. Normally when we arrived at a destination, Faith would dance in place on the rear seat of the van while waiting for the command to exit. This time she sat quietly watching me, sensing something different was about to happen.

Our test location was at the local Walmart. Clipboard in hand, a trainer-turned-tester arrived to put us through our paces. Faith and I exited the van. First task completed correctly. To my delight, Faith stayed close to me and did whatever I asked right away. Once inside the store, she sat obediently by my side while a noisy shopping cart made a circle around us. Even weaving around narrow clothing racks, she walked behind me like a pro.

I began feeling more confident. Faith and I were a team, working as one. The formidable "pretzel carry" was temporarily forgotten. Then the trainer approached a shopper with a little girl. She asked the woman if her daughter could help with our test by petting Faith. All through training, I'd had to remind Faith that socializing was off-limits during working hours. This would be hard for her.

"Faith, down." I used my authoritative voice.

She obediently lay down and stayed down while the little girl petted her.

"Good job so far," the trainer complimented. "Now go over to the counter. Buy a pretzel and have her carry it over there."

The trainer pointed to a table inside a cafeteria area connected to the store. My heart began to race, and my blood pressure surged. "That far?"

"Yes. She can do it."

"What happens if she drops it?"

"You make her pick it up and finish taking it to the table."

"What happens if I can't get her to do it?"

"You don't pass."

Nightmares of previous failures stomped through my mind as Faith and I stood in line waiting our turn. My heart raced faster the longer we waited, and I had a death grip on my wheelchair joystick. *Please, God, don't let her drop it. Don't drop it, Faith. Please, don't drop it. You can do it.*

I knew Faith felt my tension pulsing down her leash by the way she looked at me.

All too soon, the dreaded words came out of my mouth, "One regular pretzel, please. Could you put it in a bag and knot it?"

"Faith, go pay," I commanded. She took my wallet, stood on her back legs, gave it to the cashier, then sat in anticipation of its return.

"Faith, go pay," I commanded again. She retrieved my wallet and brought it to me. The time had come. I held my breath.

"Faith, go pay. Take it," I instructed, almost pleading for her to keep the pretzel bag in her mouth. As soon as the bag was in her mouth, I took off for the table before her feet touched the floor. She didn't have a chance to drop this prized possession.

Don't anybody get in my way. I'll run you over. I'll take that table. It's the closest. I must have looked like a mad woman escaping with a shoplifted pretzel, our tester running to keep up with us.

"Faith, good hold," I encouraged as our destination drew closer. And closer.

"Give! Faith, you did it!" I freely gave her praise along with a well-deserved treat. We both did our happy dance in full view of everyone. I didn't care if other people thought I was crazy. Faith was my partner.

"That was the first time she carried anything the whole distance," I told the tester in excitement.

As Faith and I relished our success, I thought I must have misunderstood the tester's next instruction, which was to place a section of the pretzel on the floor close to Faith's nose where she was lying under the table. But I followed her orders with calm aplomb. The mouth-watering delicacy had to remain within sniffing distance for five minutes without Faith acknowledging its presence. I knew she would pass this test. We were a team now!

When the time expired, I nonchalantly retrieved the pretzel. Faith's expression signaled her understanding of her success. The three of us headed back to the van, Faith prancing at my side, head held high with pride. When we reached the van, she strolled right up the wheelchair ramp and jumped on the rear seat like a pro.

The tester jotted some notes, then smiled. "You passed."

I hugged my new partner. Faith and I were now officially a team, her loyalty sealed. Though only God knew what the future held and how much more testing was to come.

Faith refusing to perform what I asked of her reminds me how frequently I ignore God when he talks to me. Too often, I'd rather live the way I want than trust him to know what is best for me. Thankfully, he waits through my stubbornness, never giving up until I'm ready to focus my attention on him.

Chapter Seven
One Wet Dog

*F*aith had endured three weeks of my lame proficiency as I learned to use commands she knew as well as did her kennel mates. We'd worked together in learning to understand each other's mannerisms. One task remained before graduation, a bath. Faith's, not mine.

This should be fun. How hard can it be to give her a bath? We're becoming a pretty good team. She has bonded to me.

All human partners were told to wear old clothing and be prepared to get wet. I wore jeans, an old top, and well-worn sneakers. I didn't care about getting wet as long as I could dry off before leaving class and exiting the building into the cool, breezy fall afternoon.

One of the trainers, Deb, led Faith and me to a large room. At the far end, staff lockers occupied one side wall. A toilet and sink on the opposite wall faced the lockers. A roll-in shower with hand-held showerhead filled the entire end of the room where we'd entered.

The three of us walked to the shower. It was guesswork deciding where to position my wheelchair so I could reach Faith without drenching the electronics on my chair. Electricity and water don't mix. I didn't want to short-circuit the chair and be left stranded.

Before starting, I removed all my jewelry, not sure how wet I might get. Then Faith's harness and collar came off but not her head halter. She always enjoyed having her harness taken off. She would roll on her back and kick her legs like a young filly in a field enjoying the fresh spring grass. Her head halter was still attached to my wheelchair by the extending leash, so her celebration was restricted. The leash allowed her to move around, but I remained in control of how far she could go.

Deb explained how I was to clean Faith's ears after her bath since past experience had taught the trainer that trying to give explanations afterward got lost in the drying activity. She then started the water and adjusted the temperature to make it suitable for Faith. Sneakers and socks came off once I realized how much water might get splashed.

Faith stood still while I received instructions on how to express her anal glands. This produced a clear, pungent fluid. *What a nasty smell!*

Dogs produced this fluid to mark territory, in response to fear and stress, or even to identify themselves to other dogs. So if this unpleasant task kept Faith for expressing herself on my home carpets, it was worth the effort—and the foul odor.

"It's now bath time," Deb said. "Go ahead and wet her down. Then put some shampoo on your hands. Rub them together before applying it to Faith. That way you won't get too much on her. The more you put on the dog, the longer it takes to rinse out. They only have so much patience when it comes to standing still for a bath."

Faith seemed to enjoy her bath. She not only stood still but turned in different directions when asked, allowing the warm water to run over her black coat and cascade to the floor. The clean, white shower floor soon sported a coating of black fur. I'd placed a towel nearby to dry her since I'd been warned she'd give a forceful shake as soon as the water stopped.

Once Faith was dry, I had to follow Deb's instructions on cleaning her ears by squirting a liquid into each ear canal to dry them out from her shower. *How can a liquid dry their ears? I wouldn't like having something cold squirted into my ear. I hope she tolerates it as well as she did her bath.*

I grabbed the towel as Deb turned off the water. I was now ready for the drying stage, but there was one problem. When I turned toward Faith, she wasn't there. She must have slipped her head halter when I turned to get the towel. I immediately spotted a sopping-wet dog frolicking back and forth around the large room, stopping every so often to shake. This sprayed water everywhere. The lockers, walls, and floor soon looked like they'd gone through the rinse cycle of a carwash.

Deb and I laughed at Faith's antics as she romped around in her unexpected freedom. The more we laughed, the more energized she got. Other teams were waiting to use the shower for their own dogs. So I needed to quickly corral her, get her under control, dry her, put her harness on, and get her back to work.

But now there was another problem. All my laughing had caused me to need the toilet facilities at the far end of the room. To give me some privacy, Deb exited. I locked the door behind her so other classmates and staff, especially the male ones, couldn't barge in on me.

My feet were too wet to put my socks and sneakers back on and the urgency too great to take the time. I drove my wheelchair to the other end of the room to access the toilet. Faith was still barreling back and forth, making it difficult to maneuver. I kept intruding into her running path, so she switched to a new game—jumping up to nuzzle me. I wasn't sure if she was saying thank you for the chance to run around while wet or she just wanted to make me as wet as her.

I used the facilities. But when I stood to readjust my clothing, my wet feet on the wet floor had no traction. The next thing I remember was finding myself sitting on the floor wedged between the wall, toilet, and wheelchair.

Faith now had me on her level and wanted to take full advantage of my predicament. She rubbed her wet body against me, then tried to bury her head in what resembled my lap. This made me even wetter than I already was. I guess she just wanted me to join her play. All I could do was laugh at my odd situation.

"Are you okay in there?" asked Deb, knocking on the door.

"I'm okay, but I fell. I'm wedged in and can't get up."

"Oh no!" Deb exclaimed. "The door's locked, and I don't have the key with me here. I'll have to go get it. Are you sure you're not hurt?"

"No, just embarrassed."

While I was trying to figure out some way to get up, I could hear muffled voices outside the door.

"Just make sure a man doesn't come to help, please," I called out. "I'm not dressed."

Silence. *Did everyone leave to help find the key?*

Time seemed to creep until I heard a key inserted into the lock. The door flung open. Deb and another trainer, Megan, hurried to my aid. They stopped short when they realized they couldn't get between the lockers and my wheelchair to help me up. They chuckled.

"You managed to get yourself into quite a dilemma," said Deb.

"I seem to get myself into predicaments frequently," I replied with a smile. "You'll have to move my wheelchair before you can get me up."

Neither Deb nor Megan were well-versed in maneuvering a power wheelchair. Depending on how they moved the joystick that manipulated the chair, they could free me of my entrapment or injure me by driving it into me.

Deb managed to move my wheelchair away. Then both ladies helped me stand and finish putting myself back together. Once I was safely in my wheelchair, we corralled Faith, put her harness back on, and went back to work as though nothing had happened.

When I recall this embarrassing event, I am reminded how reactions to such moments have an influence on our future. Our lives are filled with various circumstances, some good, some distressing. It all depends on how we view our situation as well as the attitude with which we react to circumstances. Some crises happen because of our own choices. Some from the actions and decisions of others. But God is always present to help when we allow him. Our response to each situation can make us better or bitter. Better if we learn from what happened and use it to improve our future. Bitter if we get angry at our present state, lock onto it, and allow our future to be framed by it.

Despite the challenges, the three-week training course was a wonderful experience. It ended with a formal graduation exercise of all twelve human-canine pairs attended by family, friends, and other interested parties. My husband Chas and my only sibling Eric drove down to be my guests at the event. Each human-canine team sat in the front of the room facing the audience. After receiving their diploma, the human partners were also given five minutes each to share how their dog was already changing their lives.

Graduation over, Chas and I loaded everything into the van and began the drive home to York, Pennsylvania. Faith was now a member of our family, and I looked forward to putting into practice all we'd learned within my own home and daily life.

Chapter Eight
Duty

When Faith had to go to the bathroom, she had to go no matter what weather waited to greet her. If the weather was inclement, a trip outside for Faith to do her business entailed a particularly lengthy procedure.

To begin with, my home didn't have an enclosed yard where I could just open the door and allow her to roam free until she found the perfect spot, took care of business, and came back inside. She had to be tethered to my wheelchair so distractions didn't tempt her to lose focus on why she was outside. But first, considerable preparation was necessary for both of us to brave the elements as well as to clean up the mess we'd make once we returned.

First, a stack of aged and frayed bath towels needed to be retrieved from their out-of-the-way shelf above the clothes dryer to be used as mats for my wheelchair. A long-handled gripper with a squeeze handle on one end and open claw allowed me to pull down the towels. I laid these out strategically in a line across the kitchen floor to a door leading into the yard.

The plan was to drive over them upon my return to dry my wheelchair tires. If they don't get dried, my wheelchair leaves muddy tire tracks throughout the house, squeaking all the way. The line began far enough away from the door so that when it swung open, it didn't push aside the towels, turning my carefully-laid mud extractor into a ball of useless terrycloth.

Second, I needed to prepare for the cold, wet outdoors. My body did contortions to retrieve a rain poncho from its hiding place in a bag hanging on the back of my wheelchair. Once unfolded, my next task was to place it over my head and drape it strategically over my front, the back of my wheelchair, and its arms.

I then slid plastic sleeves in which our daily newspaper arrived over the controls so they wouldn't get wet and short out the electric system, leaving me stranded outside in the elements. My purse and the utility bag attached to my wheelchair contained such essentials as my wallet, poop bags, and lipstick. I examined both bags to make sure they were closed, protecting them from becoming a soggy mess.

Now I needed to get Faith dressed to go outside. Black Labradors are water dogs who don't mind getting wet, but her leather harness had to be protected from the rain. Retrieving a large, black bag hanging on the back of my chair, I scrounged through its contents for her raincoat. This was simply a large circle of blue water-repellent cloth with two Velcro straps connecting under her belly.

Faith gave me a look that said, "Mom, do I really have to wear that?"

Indeed she did! I gave her the command to put her front paws on the seat of my wheelchair so I could better reach her. Then I draped her in the raincoat so that the patch reading *Do Not Pet Or Distract Working Service Dog* displayed prominently in the middle. The straps kept the blue material from sliding around her harness and becoming a bib instead of a raincoat. I fervently thanked the inventor of Velcro for making the process so much easier.

Last but not least, I took off my glasses since I hadn't yet found a pair of automatic wipers to keep the rain off the lenses. While my eyesight was poor without glasses, it was still better than rain-streaked lenses distorting the path to and from the bathroom area.

We were finally ready to brave the nasty weather for said duty. Attaching Faith's tether to the small ring hanging from her head halter under her chin, I pressed the button that opened the powered kitchen door. A wheelchair ramp led from the door down to the yard. Faith and I maneuvered down the slick, icy ramp at a crawl so my chair didn't try to imitate an Olympic ski jump.

But Faith had waited long enough. Her normal position when walking was at my right side. She was so desperate to reach her potty spot on the grassy area across the driveway that she rushed on past me. We rounded the end of the ramp, which faced a flower bed filled with mulch. Rather than trekking across the driveway to her normal area, Faith headed for the mulch.

"No!" I commanded.

I didn't want the flowers killed just because Faith couldn't wait a few more seconds. That this was winter and they were already dead didn't enter my brain. Faith obediently veered from the mulch, racing on ahead of me toward her intended destination. She didn't waste time sniffing for the perfect spot. As soon as her feet hit the grass, she squatted to take care of business.

Feeling much better and a little on the frisky side, Faith pranced back to me, ready to retreat to the warmth. Plastic bag in hand, I scooped up her deposit, which I dropped into a conveniently placed garbage can. Then we started back up the ramp to the warm, dry kitchen.

Oh no! The reason I'd had to go slow down the ramp was now the reason I couldn't get back up—ice! Safety and warmth teased us through the kitchen window like the sight of a brightly burning beach fire to a chilled, drowning swimmer. Fishtailing down the ramp, I tried again. No success. I slid back to the starting point. This time I put my wheelchair in slow mode before once again tackling the daunting incline. Offering a quick prayer, I made another attempt. We made slow zigzag progress, sliding our way up the ramp at a pace that would make a snail proud.

Keeping pace easily with the wheelchair, Faith kept giving me a look that communicated, "Can't you go any faster? I'm cold! I want to get inside. Why are you having so much trouble? I mean, look at me! I'm doing just fine."

We finally reached the top of the ramp. With thankfulness, I pushed the button. The door opened wide like a welcoming committee inviting us in after a long, arduous trip. The line of old bath towels lay ready to do their job. We entered fast so that the door didn't hit us as it closed.

But now my chair felt like it was plowing snow. It didn't want to move. Something wasn't right with my wheels. Looking down, I discovered a towel so tightly wrapped around one back tire it would no longer turn. *So much for taking off our soggy gear and resting from all the activity and stress!*

I fleetingly contemplated getting up and walking away from the chair. Since that wasn't possible, removing the tangled mass was my only option. But how?

Twisting my body in a contortion I didn't know it was capable of achieving, I managed to put a foot on one end of the material wrapped around my tire. With one foot stretched behind the wheelchair and my right hand on the joystick, I maneuvered my chair. Front. Left. Back. Right. The towel finally released its stranglehold on my tire and collapsed into a dirty heap on the kitchen floor.

Exhausted, I flopped against the back of my chair. Faith was so happy her mission was accomplished and her human freed of entanglement that she put her paws on my lap and licked my face. Her delight at both getting relief and being back in the warm house was evident.

"Thank you, Mom," she seemed to be saying. "I really needed to go!"

"I'm glad you enjoyed your little trek," I responded, "because I sure didn't! Maybe I should train you to use the bathroom like the rest of us. I certainly don't enjoy going outside in this mess. Next time I may just make you wait."

It was then I felt a catch in my spirit. I was reminded of the parable Jesus once told about two sons who were asked to work in their father's field. One said yes and never went while the other made excuses but eventually did as he was asked. I realized how often I make excuses when God asks me to do something. It's raining! It's too hard! It's messy!

Thankfully, God doesn't complain about helping us in our need as I'd just complained about helping my sweet, loyal canine partner in her desperation. No matter how big a chaotic shambles I create or how big the inconvenience, I can have full confidence that my loving heavenly Father will always be with me to keep me safe and clean up the mess.

Chapter Nine
Faith Knows Best

I can't breathe!" I gasped.

Thoughts of returning to the ICU formed, then faded, as the room disappeared into blackness. This wasn't supposed to be happening. After back-to-back hospital stays, I was ready to go home and stay there, not be here fighting to fill my lungs.

My first visit had occurred when my multiple sclerosis raised its ugly head and ushered me to bed, incapable of doing anything, all within a few short hours. Limbs lay dormant as though they had a mind of their own. When asked to move, they laughed at me and ignored my urgings. If my head flopped to one side, it remained there until someone turned it straight again.

Even though I'd been dealing with such episodes since 1989, this was the severest one to date. My service dog Faith eased my anxiety by lying on my bed, her warm body against me. Oxygen assisted my breathing while mega-doses of steroids coursed through my veins, their purpose to restore movement to my limbs.

The steroids did help, if only partially. My head now responded when asked to move, though this took great effort. Limbs moved in slow motion. Doctors urged me to spend time in an inpatient rehab facility to regain my strength. This would be the fastest means to return to my previous capabilities, limited as they were. I required physical, occupational, and speech therapy on a daily basis to get back my pre-episode body. Above all, I needed the ability to maneuver my power chair if I were to return to any semblance of independence.

As previously mentioned, I have an extreme allergy to latex. I discovered that some of the equipment and materials commonly used by therapists in inpatient rehab facilities were modified with latex tape. Horrifying images of experiencing a severe allergic reaction in a place meant to make me better led me to decide that the risks outweighed the benefits. Against the advice of my medical professionals, I elected to have home therapy.

Less than an hour after I arrived home, a therapist showed up to begin my rehabilitation. But an inadvertent brush with a latex bandage she was using left me taking me an emergency ride back to where I'd just left. Drawing a breath felt like sucking air through a pin-sized hole in a plastic bag. As I lay flat on my bed, tears flowed across my face and into my ears.

An ambulance was called and soon arrived. Faith looked like a Jack-in-the-Box, trying her hardest to get to me while my husband Chas worked to keep her with him. I could hear her loud cries above the emergency personnel's discussions. She couldn't understand what was happening. It was her job to take care of me, and these strangers were interfering.

Once the paramedics lifted me into the ambulance, Faith jumped right in before anyone could object. After the doors closed, she lay down quietly at my feet.

For the second time, the ICU became our home. Each day, I struggled to reach another goal. First, the oxygen became unnecessary. Rolling over in bed by myself marked my next achievement. Eventually, feeding myself could also be checked off my list. It wasn't pretty, but I got most of my food where it was supposed to go.

Recovery progressed slowly. But the day finally came for Faith and me to leave our familiar surroundings and graduate to a regular room. I laughed to myself thinking what our little parade must look like leaving the ICU. The procession members included me in my bed surrounded by mountains of belongings. One orderly was at the head of my bed, pushing it. Another was at the bottom, guiding the bed and checking for oncoming traffic when we neared a corner.

A nurse kept the IV pole close while a fourth person carried what couldn't fit on the bed. My husband Chas and Faith brought up the rear. She had to stay within eyesight of me because she took her responsibility to care for me so seriously.

It was now a year since Faith and I had been introduced to each other. During our three-week training, we'd learned how to jointly solve problems. Each difficulty we'd conquered had strengthened our bond. That bond was about to be tested.

Shortly after arriving in my new room, I asked Chas to turn on the heat. He did so. Almost immediately, I began to feel an adverse reaction. My voice turning hoarse, I asked, "Honey, do you smell something?"

"No. What does it smell like?"

"I don't know, but it's burning my throat." Suddenly, my throat closed off. I gasped out, "Honey, I can't breathe!"

Then my world turned black. I wasn't conscious when "Code Blue!" echoed through the hallways, followed by my room number. I wasn't conscious when my room filled with doctors, nurses, and special equipment, including paddles ready to shock my heart if needed. I wasn't conscious when my bed procession, followed by my husband and Faith, returned to the ICU for the third time. Or when they put me on a ventilator because I couldn't breathe on my own.

As far as I knew, I'd only slept a short time when meaningless sounds began trying to break into my peaceful world. My eyes had no reason to open, and my brain wanted to continue sleeping.

"Joan, wake up! Wake up!" a female voice echoed in my ears. "Joan, you need to wake up so we can take the feeding tube out of your nose and you can eat."

Tube? What tube? Why would I have a tube in my nose?

"Joan, you have to wake up now!"

I don't like the way you're talking to me.

The speaker's terse words finally activated my brain. The dark abyss began slowly fading away. Bright lights hurt my eyes as I forced them open. Tall, white silhouettes filled my field of vision. I wanted to retreat, but the female voice beckoned me. My eyes began to focus enough to comprehend what was in front of me, my team of doctors.

At last, I awoke enough to have the tube removed. After my room emptied, the nurses began telling me about Faith's love. Though I'd been unconscious for four days and unaware of her presence, she'd continued her vigilance. Since she was tethered to my bed, if she felt something was wrong, she'd stand up, walk to the end of her leash, and stare at the person sitting behind the nurse's counter to get her attention. Each time, the monitor at the nurse's desk confirmed something had changed in my body. Faith became their trusted change-indicator the whole time I was on the ventilator.

The IV machine that doled out my medicine sounded an alarm when the bag became empty. Faith made such a fuss the first time it happened that the nurses never allowed the alarm to go off again.

For three weeks after I awoke, Faith and I enjoyed being together in the same bed. She slept at my feet until someone entered the room. Her eyes would open to scrutinize their movements as they completed their tasks. Then she'd return to her nap.

A physical therapist came each day to exercise my weak body so I could get strong enough to go home. The time came for me to try standing at the side of my bed. This required Faith to shed her pajamas, a black mesh cape with service dog patches on it, and don her sturdy work harness. For me to accomplish my mission, Faith had to position herself where I could grab the harness handle to pull myself upright. She stood like a statue so I could keep my balance. It was her job to help me remain upright, but I had a sense Faith now viewed her work as more of a way to show how much she loved me.

Days passed as I grew stronger. People entering my room became more relaxed, a sign they knew I was improving. One day my nurse stood by my bed after she checked the IV bag and told me about life outside the hospital. Faith had been lying at my feet. She suddenly stood up and turned in a circle to change her sleeping position, then lay back down and went back to sleep. I noticed a fine mist at her back end and smelled a putrid odor.

"Ewww! What is that?" asked the nurse.

Faith had self-expressed her anal glands since I hadn't been up and around to do it for her or give her a bath. The milky substance landed on the nurse, my bed, and me. Nursing assistants hurried in to change me and the bed as well as to spray the room with deodorizer. I didn't see the nurse again until the next day.

Faith and I remained in the ICU for the duration of our hospital stay. No one wanted a repeat performance of my previous attempt to be in a regular room. The time finally arrived when the doctors decided we could once again sleep in our own beds at home.

It was approximately one year later when we learned that the strange odor in my hospital room was latex paint fumes from some remodeling that was being carried out in another part of the hospital. When the heater was turned on, this pulled the fumes into my room through the ventilation system.

Unfortunately, my latex allergy has led me to reside in the ICU a few more times since this adventure. Thankfully, I've been spared the ventilator on later incidents. For nine more years, my canine caregiver Faith was at my side during each latex event. As my MS continued to advance, she took over more and more tasks to make my life easier.

Whenever I think about my time on the ventilator with air being pumped into my lungs to keep me alive, my vision clouds with tears of deep love and appreciation for Faith. She'd watched over me steadfastly when I didn't even know she was present.

But even greater than Faith's steadfastness is our heavenly Father's, more than can even be measured. God stays with us no matter what we are going through. He cares for us all the time even when we don't know he is with us.

Chapter Ten
Habits

The process of teaching something in small steps played in my mind many times after Faith and I came home from our initial three-week training. Every routine in my life now included Faith. Routines I didn't even know I had.

There are undoubtedly many things you do each day that you don't really think about exactly how you do them or in what order. Like getting up and dressed for the day. Getting into a car and preparing to start driving. Using your microwave.

Everything changed once I had Faith to help me. I was no longer exhausted by the time I finished getting ready for the day. She brought my clothes to me, reached for my towel, and brought me my shoes and socks. Over time, we developed routines where I would give her just the first command, after which she would continue on through the normal sequence.

One sequence we learned together occurred once I'd finished my regular bathroom routine and was ready to face the day. What sounds so easy now actually took years to learn. I would say to Faith, "Let's go."

This started the sequence. It began with giving the command "side" when I was ready to leave the bathroom. Once Faith stood from her resting place on the rug and walked to my right side, I would point to a rope hanging from the door handle and give the command, "tug." After the door was open far enough for me to pass through, I would point to the light switch and say, "switch." Placing her front paws on the sink, Faith would push the light switch with her nose to turn it off.

This routine was always the same. Faith soon realized that each time we left the bathroom, the same things always happened and in that particular order. Her response became automatic. What had once taken many words, repetitions, adaptations, and patience was shortened to just two words.

One new skill for Faith was learning to turn on and off a different type of light switch. She'd been taught how to turn regular switches on and off before we were matched. During team training, we'd worked together on switches. Once we got home, I was stymied how to get Faith to turn on and off the switch in the bathroom since it has a rocker type switch instead of a regular lever. When I was unable to come up with a solution, a trainer came to teach both Faith and me how to activate this different type of switch.

Learning new things made Faith happy. She got so excited over each new skill. The more she learned, the happier she was. The happier she was, the more she wanted to learn. Our love grew stronger.

The opposite was also true. There were times when I got into a rut where I didn't have her do many things for me. When I finally did ask her to do something, she wouldn't even budge from her bed. She'd just look at me with eyes that seemed to say, "I have no idea what you are saying. You never taught me to do that."

In other words, the less she did, the less she wanted to do. Like humans, she became lazy. When this happened, I soon came to realize that learning a new skill was in order if I wanted to keep Faith sharp and on focus with her work habits.

For Faith to learn a new skill, this required breaking the skill into small steps, then repeating each step multiple times until she could execute it without any prompting from me. Depending on what new endeavor we were working on, she'd either learn it quickly or take many sessions over a period of days just to learn the first step.

One skill we worked on using when we had to cross either hot summer blacktop or salted, snowy areas. The goal was for her to place her front paws on my lap in such a way as to get her rear paws close enough so she could then place her rear paws on my wheelchair footplates. This skill enabled us to speedily cross these hazards without burning or freezing Faith's paws on the hot pavement or ice and snow.

Faith already knew the command "lap" when we met. This meant to put whatever she had in her mouth on my lap. My problem now was coaxing her to get on my lap and put her back legs on my footplates. I kept trying to think of a word other than lap. In using this different word, she'd know where to place her paws.

This may sound simple, but after three days Faith still didn't understand the difference between a regular lap and the lap needed for this skill. Nor had I come up with a different word for the command. Then I thought to simply give the "lap" command while holding a special treat at my chest. Faith eagerly got on my lap to get a treat. From then on, she grasped the difference between ordinary two-paw "lap" and four-paw "lap" with special treat. Problem solved.

The more Faith and I were together, whether learning new skills or practicing skills already learned, the more the bond between us was built up. The closer our bond, the more she wanted to please me and the more automatically I thought of her own needs and likes.

God does the same thing with us. He takes us through small steps repeatedly until what He intends us to do is learned. Then He gives something else to learn. The more we learn and do things for him, the stronger our relationship with him becomes. As our bond grows closer, we increasingly grow to love pleasing God just as Faith loved pleasing me.

Chapter Eleven
The Dirty Little Secret

S now drifted picturesquely throughout our yard. It had been unusually cold and snowy that winter. In consequence, the white, cottony flakes didn't melt like normal on the walks and driveways. My service dog Faith could find no grass to do her business. Searching for the perfect dumping ground required exploring beneath the wheelchair ramp leading up to the kitchen door or climbing to the top of a six-foot snow pile beside the ramp.

White piles of snow became dotted with brown piles. Freezing or not, removal of said waste had to be performed. Hence one very cold morning found me in my wheelchair, finagling a long-handled poop scooper through the handrail slats of the ramp while my dog watched curiously. Scooping as much snow as the sought-for prize, I was reminded of those arcade games where you line up an overhead claw over your choice of stuffed animals locked inside a glass container.

As mentioned earlier, I'd suffered from fibrocystic breast disease, which had necessitated a full mastectomy many years earlier. In consequence, I now wore breast prostheses. These were essentially a soft translucent shell filled with silicone gel molded to resemble the natural shape of a woman's breast. Originally, I'd worn these inside a special mastectomy bra with pockets that kept the two soft pouches firmly secured. But as with my shoes, I felt so much more feminine if I could wear attractive lingerie, even if no one else saw it. So I'd traded in my mastectomy bra for a less secure but far more comfortable and attractive one.

As I contorted my body downward, intent on retrieving Faith's frozen waste, the looseness of my current bra allowed one of my prostheses to slide out of its containment field and into the baggy front of the sweater I was wearing. No problem as long as I continued leaning forward, cradling my runaway neatly in the soft knit material.

By now, I'd retrieved as many piles as I could reach on the one side of the ramp. Before tackling the snow pile on the opposite side, I unthinkingly straightened my contorted body with the intention of leaning over the railing for a visual on the number of prizes available on that side. Suddenly, I heard a quiet plop. To my horror, I traced the sound to one of my prostheses, which had fallen to the ramp like an egg dropped into a frying pan.

I immediately realized what had happened. My sweater wasn't tucked into my waist, and when I'd straightened up, my runaway prosthesis had slid down my chest, out the bottom of my sweater, and onto the ramp.

My eager service dog immediately retrieved the wet, cold, and now grimy blob. Holding it in her mouth, she sat in front of me with an expression that demanded, "So what am I supposed to do with this?"

I had no answer. In its current wet, dirty state, I couldn't slip it back where it belonged. Taking the prosthesis from Faith, I placed it for safekeeping on one of my wheelchair footplates. Then I returned my attention back to the snow pile project.

My progress was abruptly interrupted by a brown UPS delivery truck that was backing into our driveway. The driver was someone I recognized since he'd often made deliveries to our home. Always friendly and smiling, he sauntered towards me carrying a box.

My brain was laboring to remember what had been ordered when my glance suddenly fell on the "egg" lying in full view on my footplate. My embarrassment conjured up a quick solution. Reaching down, I snatched up the errant object and slid it under my posterior. It sat there under me like a Whoopie cushion while I exchanged the usual pleasantries with the deliveryman.

I rejected his generous offer to carry the box inside, instead placing it on my lap. Once he returned to his truck, I immediately abandoned my original task and retreated indoors to my warm bathroom for the cleansing and reinsertion of my dirty little secret. A trip to a specialty undergarment store became top priority, where I sadly invested once again in an authentic mastectomy bra, thereby reducing any future possibility of my service dog having to hold my secret in her mouth for all to see.

We tend to live our lives the same way I treated my prosthesis. We carry our pet wrongs close to us, thinking no one will know anything about them. Then something happens to bring them into the light, and suddenly everyone around us can see our glaring fault. How much better to admit and deal with our faults instead of trying to hide them.

God knows all our wrongdoings, whether we've acted them out or kept them in the recesses of our minds. Thankfully, our heavenly Father still loves us even with all our dirty secrets.

Chapter Twelve
Faith Finds Latex

*D*o you want to learn a new game, Faith? You will get extra-special treats as a prize."

After my dangerous latex episodes, I wanted to teach Faith how to warn me if there were latex products nearby. I had met a U.S. Marshal who worked with a K-9 dog whose specialty was detecting explosives. The marshal taught me how to train Faith to sniff out latex. The process was not much different from how I'd taught Faith other new tasks.

Any training with latex had to be done outside with the help of another person. Since my episode on the ventilator, I was a little skittish about being close to any latex or smelling the fumes. A dear friend, Karen, was then and still is my aide to help me with training and other daily needs. I had her stand some distance from me holding a plastic sandwich bag packed with latex balloons.

Of course, latex balloons were not something we'd ever allowed in the house, so this was something new to Faith. Her inquisitiveness drew her to check out this new smell Karen was holding. As soon as she approached the bag, I commanded, "Faith. Latex. Sit!"

Faith had no idea what I wanted her to do, so she just kept sniffing the bag. How do you allow a dog to sniff something without touching it? She had to sniff the article to find out what it smelled like. But my allergy was so sensitive even a hint of latex proteins could send me into anaphylactic shock. If her nose touched the bag, Karen had to rub it with a handful of grass to get rid of any latex particles. For some time, Faith probably had the cleanest nose around.

One time I came up with the great idea of placing the bag on the ground and getting Faith to sniff it. She sniffed it all right. Then she promptly picked it up and began running to me, bag flapping in the breeze where it dangled from her mouth. I should have remembered there was a reason her breed is called Labrador *Retriever*. Ignoring service dog etiquette, Karen quickly grabbed Faith's harness handle to stop her. Relinquishing her prize, Faith gave me a perplexed look as she received yet another face washing.

I can imagine Faith's confusion since from puppyhood she'd been taught to pick things up and take the item to the instructor. Now I was trying to keep her from doing what her training had ingrained into her. "Let's try this again. Faith. Latex. Sit!"

Faith went straight to the bag and tried to sniff it. This time Karen pulled it out of her reach. Faith looked at me, confused. It would have been nice to work on just one part of the command at a time, but we couldn't risk it.

"Faith. Latex. Sit!" This routine repeated itself for a couple of days. Faith touched the bag while sniffing. She got her nose wiped with grass.

"Faith. Latex. Sit!" Her lack of response was frustrating. She still didn't know what I wanted from her, and I didn't know what else to try. All three of us—Karen, Faith, and I—had been working so hard with no progress.

"Faith. Latex. Sit!" I was just about to admit defeat when Faith went over to sniff the bag, looked at me, and sat.

"YEAH! You did it! You did it! You did it! I'm so proud of you. Yay!" I exclaimed, inwardly jumping up and down with excitement in my wheelchair. "Here is your extra-special treat."

Faith not only got the treat but lots of hugs and scratches. She also began springing up and down with excitement, though hers was on the outside. Karen and I were both bursting with joy. Success!

From that day on, whenever Faith smelled latex, she would sit in front of me, an intense look on her face conveying her seriousness that there was latex somewhere nearby. From the bag of balloons, she graduated to a bag of medical gloves and a piece of latex tire tubing.

We also played a game of hide and seek. Karen would hide bags containing latex around our property. Faith looked like a bloodhound as she sniffed out bushes, rainspouts, flowerpots, ornamental stones, and anything else she could reach. Because her leash was attached to my wheelchair, I would get dizzy maneuvering in circles and around obstacles to follow her so she could continue her mission. When she found the prize, she sat and stared at me, waiting for her extra-special treats that were reserved only for our latex game.

Faith became an expert at finding her latex prizes on our property, but I wondered how I would transfer her expertise to the real world. In public, I wouldn't know if latex was present until I suffered an allergic reaction. How was I going to get Faith to warn me if I didn't give her the command?

Christmas was drawing near. I needed an outdoor extension cord for the light on a nativity scene I planned to set up in our yard. So one day Karen, Faith, and I headed to the store to find what we needed. Karen was also allergic to latex though not as sensitive to it as I am. She knew the path from the store entrance to where we needed to go that would avoid bringing us in contact with latex.

This wasn't a straight line. In fact, it reminded me of the cartoon boy who gets sent on an errand and ends up traveling all over the neighborhood to accomplish it. We had to detour around the toy section, bicycles, then another detour around floor rugs, since each of these used latex rubber. Oops! We couldn't go through the bath section since bathroom rugs also have latex backing. We then detoured around the paint department. It's amazing how many things have latex.

"There's the outdoor extension cords," I finally announced with relief. "But I had no idea there were so many choices. Good grief! There must be more than a dozen here. All I want is a simple cord. How do you know the difference?"

Karen began reading labels. Their features varied widely. Each touted their product as being exactly what I needed. She and I were engrossed in our search when Faith began fidgeting. She refused to stand still, sit, or lay down as I instructed. Something wasn't right with her.

"I'm going to take Faith outside to go to the bathroom," I told Karen. "She isn't calming down, and it's been a while since I let her do her business."

The three of us left the cord aisle and started back down the main aisle. Faith immediately calmed down. She trotted peacefully at my side as I steered my power chair back through the maze to the front entrance.

"Karen, did you notice Faith?" I commented. "She's calm now. I wonder if she was trying to alert me to the presence of latex. I think I'll go back to see what she does."

"Don't you dare!" Karen objected. "If there is latex back there, do you want to provoke a reaction?"

"It's the only way I can think of to see if she was alerting me," I responded. "We'll be right back."

"And what am I going to do if you have a reaction?" Karen exclaimed.

"Get me out of here?" I suggested.

This time as I entered the extension cord aisle, I paid close attention to Faith's behavior. As I slowed my wheelchair, she came in front of me, sat, and stared right through me.

"Show me, Faith."

Faith went right to an extension cord, sat, and stared at me. She didn't touch it.

"Yes. Good girl, Faith. I'm so proud of you. Here's your special payment." I turned to my friend. "Karen, did you see that? She alerted me without the command. She caught on to what she is supposed to do. I'm so proud of her."

Tears of joy dampened Faith's black coat as I hugged and kissed her soft fur.

That incident began many years of latex alerts. I had no idea Faith would eventually save my life by consistently warning me there was danger around even before I suspected something might be amiss. One time, she even alerted me to small bags of chips on an end display in a grocery store. I brought her back to me, but she went right back to the chips, insisting there was latex on the display.

"Faith, there is no latex in chips," I scolded her. "I don't understand why you keep alerting me."

By this time, a store employee had come over to see if she could help us. I explained what Faith was doing and why. At first, she was shocked that Faith could detect latex and as stumped as I was. But as we chatted, we realized that whoever had packaged the chip bags into boxes for shipping may have worn latex gloves. The employee got what I needed, and I avoided the area from then on.

Faith's sensitive nose warned me of danger long before my own nose detected anything or my body reacted. Though I can't see latex particles in the air, I could trust Faith to keep me safe by telling me when this dangerous-to-me substance is close by.

Similarly, God can't be seen either, but I trust him to keep me safe. He alerts us to danger, but sometimes we ignore him or don't understand what he is telling us. The only way to know for sure is to stay in close communication with him. In order to do that, you need to read the letters he has written to us, i.e., God's Word. Just as Faith had to practice with me to know what latex was and how to alert me, so we need to practice knowing what our heavenly Father is telling us by reading the Bible.

Chapter Thirteen
Push the Panic Button

I acquired one of those HELP-I'VE-FALLEN-AND-CAN'T-GET-UP buttons. It resembled a gray, rectangular faceless watch and could be worn two different ways. One way was as a necklace dangling from a black cord, definitely not my fashion style. The other option was to use the hook-and-loop nylon strap to wear it on my wrist. This functioned well as long as I didn't mind snagging just about anything that came in contact with it or having it adhere itself to my wrist. All was solved once I purchased a watch band to replace the catching strap. People never even noticed my new bracelet.

The button didn't work unless a base unit received its signal. The installer placed the tan box with its red button and gray lever next to a landline phone on an organizer stand beside the dining room table. The unit looked innocent sitting there doing nothing except for the glow of a small, green light and two phone cords coming out of it. One cord went to the phone right beside it. The other cord draped over the edge of the organizer stand onto the floor, where it snaked under the table to the other side and plugged into a phone jack mounted on the wall at floor level.

"What is the gray lever for?" I asked the installer.

"If you are near the unit or someone else needs to call for help, just push the lever," the man explained. "This will automatically connect a call to our center. They will contact you through this unit to see if you are all right. If you don't answer their callback, they will immediately call whatever emergency contacts you've given us and make sure that help is immediately sent to you."

"I have a service dog and would like to teach her to use it," I said. "But the center of the button I wear is recessed. She won't be able to push it."

"It's recessed to reduce accidental calls."

"She also can't reach the base unit to press the lever. Is there something you can do so she can call for help if I can't?"

"I'll see what I might be able to do," he responded graciously.

By the time he was finished, a silver push plate like those used to open doors in public places had been positioned on the wall at doggie nose height. My next challenge was to teach Faith how to push it hard enough with her paw to activate the unit. I also had to decide which word to use as a command so she knew what to do. To her, this would be a new game with lots of treats.

"Faith, touch," I told her.

She knew what touch meant and hit the plate. Nothing happened.

"Faith, touch." Same result, nothing.

"Faith, touch." I guess she'd had enough of this new game. She hit the push plate so hard I thought it was going to come off the wall.

"Your call is being connected. Please wait," a robotic monotone announced from the base unit. "Your call is being connected. Someone will be right with you."

"Faith, you did it! Yay!" We celebrated her success.

A short time later, an actual human voice spoke from the base unit. "This is your help line. Joan, do you need help?"

"No thank you. I'm just teaching my service dog how to press the button to get help."

"That is great. Do you need help?"

"No, I don't. But thank you."

"Before I go, are you sure you don't need help?"

By now I was wondering if she had decided to play a game called, "Do You Need Help?"

"No. I don't need help."

"Everything is coming in loud and clear. I'll reset the connection. You have a good day."

"You have a good day also."

Hitting the panic button had caused the little green light on the base unit to turn off. Now a beep sounded, and the green light came back on. Looking down at Faith, I commented thoughtfully, "You know, this is going to be a long process if we have to go through this conversation every time you push that button."

Faith looked at me with her head tilted as if to say, "I know what you mean."

We got into a routine. Faith would hit the push plate with her paw. We'd wait for someone to answer, then I'd make sure they understood I didn't need any help. They'd reset the connection, and we'd start all over again. All this took time. I was never going to get Faith to understand the urgency of immediately pushing the plate if there was so much time between each practice run.

I got the brilliant idea to look at the owner's manual. Right there in black and white, it gave instructions on how to test the unit. If I held the lever down on the base unit until it announced test mode, we had a couple minutes to work on this new process.

It didn't take long for Faith to learn what she was to push. Then I had to think of a different word so that she knew it meant to push *that* particular plate. She also had to do it in a hurry. I came up with the word "help."

"Faith, touch, help."

Faith obediently pressed the plate.

"Faith, touch, help." She pressed it again. Each time, she got quicker on her response. That meant she was learning what to do without having to think about it. I could now drop the work "touch."

"Faith, help." She looked at me as if to say, "I don't know what 'help' means."

"Faith, help." I paused, then repeated, "Faith, help."

My tone expressed the urgency. Faith stood in front of me, her facial expression indicating she was thinking hard about what help meant. Her expression suddenly changed as the lightbulb of understanding blinked on. Running to the push plate, she hit it hard with her paw.

"Yay! You did it!" We both celebrated with hugs, treats, and scratches. I hugged. She got the treats and scratches.

Each training after that, Faith would run to the push plate and press it if I called, "Faith, help." As long as she was in eyesight of the button, she raced to do her duty. But if I was in a different room where she couldn't see both me and the plate, she didn't like leaving me. Eventually, the lure of receiving her treat for completion of this new skill would win out.

It was now time to take this training to the next level. I arranged to prop open the door leading outside to the ramp I used to get down to ground level and back up to the house door. Steering my wheelchair outside to the top of the ramp, I gave the command. She hesitated, then raced back inside the house to her goal.

I took her next a short distance down the ramp and repeated the command. Instead of racing to the push plate, she disappeared down her special steps attached to the side of the ramp. Deaf to my calling, she opted instead for a bathroom break. Intermission over, it was back to work.

This time I strategically placed my aide Karen to block Faith's special steps so there would be no repeat performances, then took Faith all the way to the end of the ramp. When I gave the command, she raced up the ramp. But once she reached the landing where the ramp makes a hard left up to the house door, she would go no further. She ran up and down the ramp, but no amount of verbal prodding could get her to abandon her station for her push plate reward.

After calling her back, Karen and I began the segment again. She shot up the ramp, only to go no further than the last time. This time,

I maneuvered my wheelchair back up the ramp toward her while more urgently expressing the command, "Faith, help. I need help!"

This only increased her stress level. Racing to the open doorway, she halted on the threshold as though at an invisible wall. Going no further, she looked through the railing slats at me, her panicked eyes conveying her fear of what I was asking. Then she turned around, her paws barely touching the ramp as she fled back to me. She hesitated momentarily when she reached Karen, her intense brown eyes looking up at Karen as though pleading, "Please help my mommy! She needs help!"

I had to do something that would allow Faith to feel success while relieving the stress this was causing her. Her frantic running back and forth was wearing an indentation in the ramp's wood flooring. I started moving up the ramp closer and closer to her. But my closeness made no difference in encouraging her to carry out her task until I reached the "invisible wall" of the open doorway. Racing inside, she pushed the plate, then dashed back to me.

"You did it, Faith. You did it. I'm so proud of you."

Treats, hugs, praise, belly scratches, and tail wags ended our session. Tears wet my cheeks as I recognized her love and dedication. In her eyes, I was in trouble, so she desperately wanted to get help for me. But she was also not about to abandon me.

In the end, she never did learn to go inside and push the plate if I was outside in the yard. She simply could not bring herself to abandon me even to get help. Though learning this new skill wasn't a total success, it was a sweet reminder of how God has promised he will never leave us or forsake us. Far more than even the most faithful service dog, he loves me beyond measure and is fully dedicated to my wellbeing.

Do I ignore him at times, thinking my way is better? Sadly, I do. Oh, to have such a deep love for my heavenly Father that like my devoted Faith I can't bear to be away from him for even a moment.

Chapter Fourteen
In the Dark

A free one-week vacation at the beach. Who could refuse? Me, maybe. I am not a big beach fan. I don't particularly care for it, but it sure likes me. It likes to stick really close. So close I can't get it off. Besides, did you ever try to get wet sand off a dog?

The beach vacation was actually the senior trip for the Christian school where I'd taught and where my husband was still employed. Chas had been this group's class advisor since their freshman year of high school. Now we were invited to accompany them as they spent the money they'd worked so hard to raise for the last four years.

The group would be divided between two beach houses, one for the girls and one for the boys, both belonging to a resort within easy walking distance to the beach. But my excitement at the prospect faded as memories of previous such excursions rose to the surface. While the houses chosen looked luxurious in the rental catalog, they were not handicapped accessible. Each beach house consisted of three floors of bedrooms, bathrooms, game rooms, dining area, and one kitchen. The main rooms were typically on the second and third floors due to elevated water levels during storms. This meant steps. Many steps.

They were also usually steep, carpeted, narrow, and sometimes spiraled to create a breathtaking visual effect. Though not quite the same kind of breathtaking for me. Wheelchairs don't do steps. This meant I'd be relegated to a small first floor bedroom. It would be easy enough to go for a walk—or rather power chair drive—along the water or head to the beach for a swim. But if I wanted to eat or socialize with others in our party, someone would have to carry me up to the second or third floor dining area, wherever it might be located in that particular house.

Nightmares from past class trips of being carried up and down stairs started playing through my memory. Getting from one floor to another entailed one sturdy, straight-backed chair and three or four strong young men. I'd chuckled inwardly as I listened to them strategizing how to accomplish their assignment without giving me a close-up view of the stairs below. Of course, they wouldn't accept suggestions from me. After all, they were seniors, and there were girls to impress.

You can just imagine sitting in a chair with no seatbelt and trusting your life to four novices as they maneuver a winding, narrow staircase. They might have successfully completed a year of calculus or physics, but now they had to apply in real life what they'd learned on paper. Except there'd be no erasing and starting over to correct a mistake.

One of my more petrifying memories was of a set of narrow stairs encased with walls on both sides. To add interest, the stairs switched directions halfway up at a landing. I was entrusting my life to young muscles insecure about what they were doing. Once started, they couldn't stop in the middle to decide on a different strategy because there was no place to put down the chair. The view from my chair included bulging arm muscles on either side of me and heavy breathing as my porters strained to make any progress.

At first, I was glad their bulk shielded me from the full perilous view of those steep stairs until I spotted Faith below me, frantic at what she saw. She was in charge of me, and she didn't like seeing me in such a predicament, I began wondering if maybe she knew something I didn't.

All of a sudden, my view of Faith and the steps we'd just climbed came closer and closer. My body tilted sharply forward, and my heart rate rose. Fast.

"Augh!" I yelled, fearful of being catapulted off the chair and landing on Faith below. "Tip me back! Tip me back!"

The boys tipped me back but had nowhere to set me down so they could regroup. Finally, they managed to get me to the top of the stairs. It had been a close call, but they improved with each new trip up and down the stairwell. No more close calls.

Another senior trip involved using the same method of carry except that all my trips were outside. This was because the inside staircase had been configured in such a manner that carrying a chair was not possible. Instead, my teenaged porters had to carry me up a winding outdoor staircase to the third floor, where a door led into the kitchen. From the bottom, this looked romantic, the wooden stairs enveloping the house like a curling vine as it rose from the ground floor to the third floor. I'm not sure who was more anxious as we ascended the outside staircase, the boys out of fear of dropping me or me remembering previous excursions upstairs.

As we ascended, my view intermittently changed from the twilight sky to the spot-lit ground below. I held my breath, though I'm not sure why. I doubt it made me any lighter, and I certainly couldn't hold it the whole trip.

"I'm . . . getting tired," one of the boys exhaled. "Can we . . . rest for a minute."

"No!" another boy informed him. "There's no place to stop. Keep going."

These were not comforting words. By the time we reached our destination, the boys were gasping for air, whether from exertion, fear, or both. My heartrate gradually returned to normal along with my blood pressure. Faith greeted me with her usual in-my-face excitement, having been brought up the inside steps by Chas.

In some ways, I felt like a queen being carried on her royal throne. In other ways, I felt like an experiment with the object being to get the baggage up and down safely without losing it.

As I continued mulling over these harrowing memories, Chas interrupted my trance. "Hey, you might want to know the house where we'll be staying has an elevator."

"Yay! Tell them thank you, thank you, thank you so much!"

I was so touched by the class's thoughtfulness. No more wooden chair escapades. No more nightmares of steep staircases. Maybe this senior class had heard what previous classes had to go through and decided an elevator was safer for me. Or maybe the male members of the class just didn't want to try to carry me. Either way, Faith and I were grateful. We'd be able to access the other floors whenever we wanted. Be with the other girls. I'd never been able to do that. What a blessing!

Once we got there, I was so excited to see my conveyance. As usual, the class was divided between two beach houses, one for the boys and one for the girls. The one with the elevator had been assigned to the girls, along with Chas, Faith, and me. I made sure to thank the students for spending their hard-earned money to make traveling between floors possible. The seniors enjoyed having an elevator in the house, too. All the girls' luggage and myriad food boxes could be taken to other floors with the push of a button.

"I'm so glad we have an elevator in the girls' house," I heard one boy say. "I wouldn't like to carry all this kitchen stuff to the third floor by stairs."

"I wish we had an elevator in our house," another boy added. "It sure would make life easier."

Each time Faith pushed the button to call the elevator, I thanked God for the blessing of independence. Up to the third floor. Down to the second. During that week, Faith and I visited each floor and engaged in conversations impossible in previous years. I got to know the students as people rather than names my husband would talk about. The week passed fast. Time to go home.

Faith and I were asked if we'd be willing to leave a day early with some of the students. I rushed through sorting stacks of clothes, books, and dog essentials I'd placed around our room in a logical way. My husband's things needed to stay. At least if he wanted to have anything to wear. Faith could see something was happening and showed her disapproval by pacing.

As much as I was grateful for this means to access each floor, the elevator was a bit on the small size. To use this conveyance, I had to back my chair in with the footplates up. Then Faith backed into the long, narrow space between the wall and my chair. Anything else had to sit on my lap. Faith didn't like the multiple trips crammed with suitcases, doggy bags, incidentals, and us.

"It's a good thing neither one of us is claustrophobic," I told her. "We'd never have used this elevator."

By now I was tired from all the last-minute frenzy of packing up Faith and myself, followed by multiple elevator rides. "Last trip, Faith. All we have left is a small bag and my pillow. It sure would be nice to have an elevator in our own house, wouldn't it? Though maybe a little bigger."

Faith tilted her head to look up at me, clearly saying, "Mom, I really don't like riding in this thing."

We entered the elevator using a by now well-practiced routine. I placed my pillow between my headrest and the elevator wall. Then I pulled the main door closed and latched, followed by a gate that looked like a metal wall of diamond shapes as it expanded across the opening, much like a collapsible baby gate. I'd learned by experience that the elevator wouldn't move if not latched properly.

"Here goes, Faith. Our last trip." Pushing the button, I leaned back against my pillow to relax. The motor hummed as our tight cubicle descended for the last time. Then the elevator stopped.

"That didn't take as long as I'd have thought," I commented to Faith. "I guess my attention was more on going home."

I started opening the door. Or so I thought. It acted like it was glued shut. I pushed the button to go back up and try again. No go. I tried not to panic. How would we get out of this packed box? I yelled, but the sound only hurt my ears as it reverberated in the enclosed space. We were stuck.

Faith began to get restless. She could tell something wasn't right and felt my anxiety growing. At least there was a light so I could read until others realized something was wrong. That would relieve my nervousness.

But before I had a chance to get my book out, we were plunged into complete blackness. Not a sliver of light anywhere. I'd never experienced anything like it. In fact, it was so dark I became disoriented and had to hold onto my chair to keep from falling out of it. My anxiety grew, and Faith became more restless. She needed to calm down, but I couldn't see where to reach to touch her for reassurance.

"Well, Faith, I'm not sure what to do now." I leaned down to feel for her, but finding her proved harder than I expected. The wall wasn't where I thought it was. I slammed my hand against it, then slid it down until I found Faith's soft fur. I stroked it gently, trying to calm both of us, but my fear remained.

The complete lack of light reminded me of where Scripture states that those who don't know Christ are cast into outer darkness. If that was anything like this, the utter inability to know where I was or see anything, even my hand in front of my face, I was relieved that I would never experience such. Knowing Christ meant that I would spend eternity with him.

How do we get to know Christ? By dealing with the wrongs in our lives. If we have done anything wrong ever, we will not be accepted into heaven. Those wrongs are like a debt. Before we can move on, that debt must be paid. There is no way we can pay our own way into heaven, but there is someone who has already paid our debt. Christ paid the debt for everyone's wrongs. We need to believe and accept his payment for our wrongs in order be with him when we die.

There was no point in letting myself be consumed with fear, so I decided it was nap time. My lap was full of stuff, but I managed to position my pillow to rest my head. I spoke toward where my touch had told me Faith was crouched down.

"Faith, I'm not sure how you'll sleep. You're already cramped with all the stuff in here. But I'm taking a nap until help comes."

I received no response. For all I knew, Faith might already be sleeping. Just as I leaned my head back against my pillow, I heard muffled voices. "Mrs. P. Are you in there?"

I rattled the metal gate that stood sentry between the main door and me.

"Hurry up, Mr. P." I recognized the voice as one of the students. "I found your wife. She's stuck in the elevator."

What I heard next was a frenzy of activity. It sounded like everyone in the house was outside the elevator trying to get it open. Faith stirred, probably in anticipation of freedom. By now, unfortunately, I'd made another revelation. While the house was air conditioned, the elevator shaft was not. It was also sealed tight. Take a very small area, insert one human plus one large dog giving off lots of heat, and very quickly it becomes a sauna.

Then a different voice entered the scene. I strained to hear what sounded like the maintenance man for the resort community. Here was someone who was surely trained to open the door. Finally!

But trained or not, he wasn't successful. I could hear the man say something about doing what the elevator installers told him. My anxiety became more intense, which meant Faith got more restless. The longer he tried, the more panicked his voice. My anxiety turned into full panic. Would Faith and I grow old together in our little cube? What if I had to go to the bathroom?

More voices entered the cacophony already voicing opinions on how to get the door off. These voices asked questions about the mechanics of the door. The response to each was, "We tried that." Authoritative or not, they weren't any more successful than anyone else.

I slouched down in my chair. I was beginning to experience breathing difficulties due to the increased temperature. Heat is no friend to multiple sclerosis. The hotter I got, the weaker my body became until I felt like a marionette with broken strings. Faith had been quiet for some time. I figured the heat was getting to her as well. My brain wanted to panic even more for her, but it took too much effort.

Then suddenly, blinding light and cool air washed over me. Once the elevator door was open, I could see the elevator had only traveled about eight inches from where it had started. Stepping forward, my husband immediately saw that I was in distress.

"I'll lift her legs," he called out. "Someone else lift her torso to get her out of there. I think she's passed out from the heat."

With those words, I could feel him lift my legs. But whoever was going to carry my torso never got to do it. Like a cartoon character, my body slithered out of my chair onto the floor.

"Are you hurt?" voices asked anxiously. "Do you feel any pain?"

I was laughing too hard to answer. All I could think about was what I must have looked like. What a dramatic entrance into a room I discovered to be filled with paramedics, mechanics, chaperones, and students.

Faith was so excited to be out of confinement she wanted to play. She didn't act like she'd been trapped in a dark, tiny space. Even though the students knew she was on duty so shouldn't be petted, she made her rounds excitedly, thanking them in her doggy way.

My memory is a bit fuzzy as to what followed. I am told the paramedics switched into trained medical mode. They performed the normal procedures to ascertain my condition. Next, they cooled my body by placing ice packs in strategic places. What an extreme! I began to shiver.

"Ma'am, we are going to transport you to the hospital to get checked out," said one paramedic.

"No, I don't want to go."

"You've been through a trauma. You need to be checked out to make sure everything is okay."

"I'll be fine. Just let me sleep it off. There are enough people here to get help if I need it."

In the back of my mind, I knew the paramedics were right, but I was too tired to go through any more jostling. My brain wanted to turn off any unnecessary thinking, including answering the myriad of questions I'd have to answer if taken to the hospital. And Faith had been through this with me. She needed to be near me in a comfortable setting, not in an ambulance and whatever else would follow. Besides, taking me to the hospital would pose a huge inconvenience on the rest of the group.

"We can keep a close watch on her," one chaperone spoke up. "Her husband is here too. Between all of us, she'll be in good hands."

Finally convinced I was going nowhere, the paramedics made sure to register their displeasure about not taking me to the hospital before packing up their equipment and leaving. For the rest of the day, I felt like a queen. Every few minutes, one of the students popped their head in the door to see if I wanted anything. Dinner and breakfast were served in bed.

The next day, I was offered plenty of help repacking in anticipation of leaving with everyone else. As several students escorted me to the elevator, I said, "Okay, time to try this again. Though I'm a little leery about getting into that elevator. Is it really fixed? The last time I saw it, the door was lying on the floor."

"All fixed," I was assured. "We'll help you at the top, and someone else will be waiting at the bottom."

Faith entered the elevator as though nothing had happened the day before. She was so brave to trust me to keep her safe. I went through the process of securing the door and gate, then pushed the button, hoping this time the motor would continue its descent.

In no time, the door flung open. Faith and I were met by many happy faces. The students helped us get into the bus to go home. While the end of our week hadn't turned out quite the way I'd expected, that experience has become one of my most memorable

.

Chapter Fifteen
Circus Act

"Faith, want to go play?" I asked my service dog as the ramp extended from my van. Her lunge into the back seat in near record time gave her answer. When she heard the word play, she complied with commands without hesitation because she knew fun time was coming.

Chas, my husband, accompanied us to the local park for some fresh air and change of scenery. Our destination atop a grassy hill overlooking the Susquehanna River created the ideal backdrop for ball throwing and retrieving. Chas picked out a shady spot under the closest pavilion to relax and read.

Meanwhile, I began undressing Faith from her service dog gear. This had to be executed in sequential order or she'd be off and running with half her uniform still on. I'd learned that little nugget by experience. Trying to get her to stand still while attempting to get the rest of her gear off would be like trying to catch a lightning bug blindfolded.

First to come off was her power steering mechanism, the head halter around her nose where a leash attaches. Next came her pink scarf, worn so people would know she's a girl. Lastly, her harness was removed. When people first met Faith, they often wondered why she had to wear the halter.

"Why does she have a muzzle on?" they'd ask. "Does she bite?"

"It's not a muzzle," I explained. "It's like a bridle on a horse. I can guide her more easily by her nose than by her neck."

I'd tell people Faith had an invisible wire between her ears. She'd stand still while getting undressed until the halter and harness passed over her ears. This tripped the wire. She'd immediately drop to the ground and roll on her back, wiggling and kicking the air. The impression she gave was that of a woman expressing how good it felt to take off her bra.

This routine completed, Faith placed her front paws on my lap and nuzzled for her ball. "Mom, I want to play," she conveyed. "Where's the ball?"

Canine Partners for Life had a rule about playing in areas that aren't fenced in. The dog must be attached to a rope so they can't run after anything that catches their interest. In this area of the park, Faith would have lots of wildlife to distract her, so I hooked one end of the rope to Faith's collar. Holding the other end, I sat looking at my expectant girl.

"Okay Faith. Now where am I going to tie the other end? There's nothing but grass around here. Do you think I can tie it around my waist? Sure, why not! After all, what could happen? I weigh a whole lot more than you do."

Our playtime routine began. Number one: throw the ball. Number two: Faith races for ball. Number three: Faith catches the ball and races back to me. Number four: Faith relinquishes her treasure in my lap, ready for a repeat performance.

"I wonder how long this rope is," I commented when she'd once again dropped the ball into my lap. "You've run quite far and haven't yet extended the rope the full length. Of course, you don't have to test it. I was only curious."

I guess Faith wanted to find out too. The next throw answered my questions and confirmed the laws of physics. Number one: objects in motion tend to stay in motion. Number two: objects rolling downhill tend to increase speed.

It all started when Faith missed my throw. Not wanting the ball to escape down the grassy knoll out of her reach, she pursued her prize with gusto. The rope began uncoiling to its full length. What happened next occurred in slow motion, at least in my perception. I felt my body leave my wheelchair. Arms and legs freed from their wheelchair confines stretched out in different directions. Pulled after the running dog, my body lurched through the air as though I'd been shot out of a circus cannon.

The flight lasted at least a whopping second or two. My four-point landing, two arms and two knees, would definitely not have qualified for the Olympics. Thankfully, nothing seemed to be broken. The situation was so humorous I rolled over in sheer laughter, wondering if any observers liked my circus act debut.

Chas ran to my rescue from the pavilion where he'd been engrossed in a book. "Are you okay? Are you hurt?"

I sat up. "The only thing hurt is my pride."

Excited I was on her level for a change, Faith bathed my face with her tongue kisses. Ball throwing had to be temporarily suspended until I could get back in my chair and examine myself for any hurt injuries. I found none, only grass stains on my knees where I'd landed.

Chas removed the rope from my waist, his expression making clear he wasn't happy with my performance and didn't want a repeat. He fastened the rope to a better anchor on my wheelchair so there'd be no chance of practicing my flight and landing routine.

"I thought it looked dangerous having the rope around your waist," he commented tersely. "I should have said something. I didn't even think of you flying through the air."

Faith had no idea I'd been in any danger, and I too had been oblivious to what might happen. It was a reminder of how often we put ourselves in situations where we have no idea the cost our actions could have on our relationship with God. We anchor our hopes and dreams on people, jobs, or situations that might help us achieve them. What we need to remember is that God is the only anchor that holds onto us no matter what happens or where we end up.

Chapter Sixteen
A Very Long Plane Ride

O ur family headed to Alaska for a once-in-a-lifetime cruise. I was excited to see our nation's largest state but fearful because this would be Faith's first flight. There would be no room for errors when executing a command or for Faith deciding she wasn't in the mood to work.

To prevent her from having to go to the bathroom while in the air, Faith wasn't allowed any food or water the morning of travel. After all, to the best of my knowledge, planes didn't have anywhere for dogs to find the right blade of grass outside the airplane at thirty thousand feet in the air.

The anticipated morning arrived. First on my list was taking Faith outside to go to the bathroom, which as I've shared in a previous chapter takes far less time than my getting ready to take her outside. Bladder and stomach empty, she normally races back inside to her food dish and obediently sits until I release her to eat one of her two meals for the day.

On this morning, Faith's facial expression communicated, "Hey, you forgot me! Where's my breakfast? Where's my bowls?"

"I can't feed you today," I explained. "We are going on a long plane ride, and there is no bathroom for you on the plane. I know you have no idea what I'm saying. All you want is breakfast."

I had to leave or her eyes would have dissolved my resolve. She followed me as I steered my wheelchair around the house, clipboard in hand, checking off each last-minute item as it went into a suitcase.

"Feed me," her eyes communicated pleadingly. "I'm hungry!"

Faith could tell something was happening. First, no breakfast and no water. Now her favorite blanket disappeared into the same suitcase as her food and drink bowls. I was going to ask Faith to bring me her toy, but then she'd expect playtime to follow, so I lifted it out of her basket. She kept her eyes glued on the toy as I dropped it into her suitcase. This was already stuffed with eleven days of meals. Earlier in the week, she'd stood sentry while meal-sized portions were scooped from the gray plastic tub of dog food into zip-lock bags for easy delivery while traveling.

When Faith could take the abnormal activity no longer, she either lay on her bed or sat in some strategic location watching Mommy scurry around, her anxiety palpable.

Chas crowded our suitcases plus Faith's bag into the car once I'd zipped them shut for the last time. Trying to pack all our clothing, personal products, medical supplies, and Faith's things into the allowable number of bags while keeping them under the maximum weight was like trying to put a jigsaw puzzle together with pieces that kept changing.

I also had to figure out which bags would be carry-on and which would get checked. Nightmares of our luggage taking a vacation in Hawaii instead of Alaska made me want to take all of it as a carry-on, especially Faith's bags. She would be without any food until we landed in Alaska, and I certainly wanted to be sure she had something to eat when we got there.

Once everything was crammed in the car, we were finally ready to leave. Faith obediently walked up the van ramp, jumped onto the back seat, and lay down, giving a humph to make sure I knew of her displeasure.

"That's enough, Faith. You don't need to do that," I chided as I attached her seatbelt to her harness. Next stop the airport.

I was already exhausted from the frantic packing marathon. As we pulled to the curb at our airline's designated place, my blood pressure and pulse rose. Vehicles pulled up to the curb, vomited their contents onto the sidewalk, and pulled back into traffic. All within a matter of a few eye blinks. To empty our van meant unloading all the luggage and Faith. Then I'd need to transfer from my car seat to my wheelchair, drive down the ramp, and wait for the ramp to fold back into place and the door to close. All this took time. Lots of time.

As soon as we parked, helpful hands started grabbing luggage and putting it on a dolly. Faith was glad to be out of her cramped quarters but not sure of her surroundings.

"Sir, my husband has to park our car," I told the baggage porter loading our possessions. "Where do I go until he comes back?"

"I'll push your luggage to the back, and you can wait here for him."

"Thank you so much. I have no idea what we are doing or how to get to where we need to go next."

"Just go through those doors, and the check-in desk is straight in front of you."

"Thank you."

Faith and I accompanied our luggage to the rear of the organized chaos to wait. My vital signs began to return to normal as I watched other baggage porters assist new arrivals and send them on to the next stop in the boarding process. There was nothing that seemed to perplex them as they retrieved some odd baggage, put it on dollies, and answered the same questions over and over again with a courteous smile.

Once Chas returned from parking, we headed inside. Check-in desk, here we come! The line to the counter serpentined from the door we'd come through all the way to the counter. Repeatedly, we moved all our belongings, stood still, moved again, stood still. The closer we got, the faster my heartbeat. All our careful packing was about to be tested.

Chas placed the first bag on the scale. I held my beath.

"Sir, your bag is two pounds overweight. Do you want to pay the overage charge?"

"Please weigh the other one."

"That one is under. You can take your bags aside and rearrange them."

Talk about airing out your laundry. In the presence of all curious eyes lay our two largest bags. Taking two pounds out of one was easy. It left a nice-sized hole. The hard part was finding something the size of that hole to go into it and even out the weight.

"Your CPAP is what weighs so much," I said to Chas. "But there isn't room in the other bag."

A voice spoke up from behind the counter. "You may take as many medical bags as you need on the plane."

"Thank you," I responded. *I wish we'd known that sooner!* I thought through my pasted-on smile.

Bags zipped, weighed, tagged, and on the conveyor belt, they headed on their way to the plane. Now it was our turn to head onward to security. We stood in the long line, waiting for the privilege to pass under the gray metal arch, not the golden arches. I observed people practically undress and place everything in a gray tub, then watch it disappear behind black strips of rubber, only to reappear intact on the far side.

"I wonder what they are going to do with Faith and me," I said to Chas.

"Well, you certainly can't go through the scanner. I'm guessing they'll have to do it another way, probably take a wand over you and Faith."

"I hope Faith behaves and doesn't get excited or jittery. Either way, it could make things difficult for the examiner, which could get us in trouble." Visions of Faith and me being hauled off to jail because she wouldn't cooperate crossed my mind.

"Well, at least now I know why we're told to report two hours before flight time. If we went any slower, we'd be going backwards."

Faith didn't like getting comfortable on the cool floor, only to get up, move a few feet, and stop again. But we finally reached the checkpoint. A security officer addressed my husband. "Sir, place your belt, shoes, and contents of your pockets in a tub and place it on the conveyer belt."

"What about my wife's bags?" Chas asked.

"You'll have to take them all off her chair and send them through in a tub."

I hadn't thought about this part of security.

"It's not all that easy. Can we do something else?" I asked the security officer.

"No. They must come off."

It had been a long time since the straps holding my two bags onto my wheelchair had been removed. I wasn't even sure how each one was intertwined around the pieces of my chair to hold the bags at just the right location for easy access. My husband certainly had no idea how untangle them. *Great, now we are holding up everyone else from getting to their gate on time!*

"You should have taken them off before we got here." Chas's waning patience was showing.

My frustration surfaced. "I had no idea I'd have to, or they'd have been off by now."

Once the spaghetti straps of my purse and bag were unwound from my chair, they were placed in tubs moving through the X-ray machine. Yes, tubs. My wheelchair makes an excellent pack horse. I've been told I carry everything on my chair but the kitchen sink.

If I ever find a small sink, it's going in there too. After all, I need to be prepared for any emergency that might happen.

Chas managed to get through the arch in one beep (belt buckle). Faith and I were escorted to an area between the arches. Still quite visible to everyone.

"I'm going to lightly run my hands down your arms and legs," the security officer told me. "Now please lean front so I can feel down your back."

The officer then attached a small piece of cloth to a plastic stick. "Now I'm going to move this wand over your brace." She brushed the stick against the brace I wore to hold up my foot. "Okay, you are free to go."

"Aren't you going to check my dog?" I didn't want to have problems later.

"No, I don't want to disturb her."

"Go ahead. She is trained to stand still."

Faith stood like a statue as the officer checked her harness and other gear, looking at me as if to say, "What is she doing? Is she finished?"

The officer finally declared us clear to proceed to the waiting area at the gate. At that point, an airline employee approached us and announced, "Please follow me. We want to get you onboard and settled before others board."

Thunk. Thunk. Thunk. That was the sound my wheelchair made every time it went over a seam in the tunnel leading to the plane. Faith wasn't sure what was happening but trotted by my side.

At the plane's entrance, I had to transfer from my wheelchair to a special skinny aisle chair to maneuver between the rows so personnel could move me to our seats. Two strong male orderlies, one in front of me and one in back, were lifting me out of my chair when Faith began to get very upset. She kept pulling on the leash Chas was holding, trying to get to me. Between her antics and crying, she sounded as though she thought I was being attacked. No matter what I said, she didn't like anyone else doing anything to me. I was her charge, and she took her responsibility seriously. No one else was allowed to do her job.

Once I was settled in my seat, Faith nudged me repeatedly, making sure I was all right. Satisfied, she calmed down. I removed her harness to give her more room at my feet. By now a steady flow of passengers were shuffling past her, finding their seats, and stuffing belongings in the overhead bins. Faith now considered me to be safe, so she curled in a tight ball at my feet, content for the time being.

Faith quickly became the attention of those around us, including the flight attendants. Because of space constrictions, we couldn't perform our normal mini-demonstration, but I fielded many questions.

"Where does she go to the bathroom?" asked one flight attendant.

"She doesn't. That's why she hasn't had anything to eat or drink since last night."

"Poor dog! She must be starving and thirsty."

"Yes, but she'll be okay once we get to Alaska. Then I can feed her and give her a drink."

"May she have some ice?"

"Sure. She loves to chew on ice."

"Good. I'll see what I can do once we're in the air and serving beverages." The flight attendant kept her word. Each time the beverage cart passed, chips of ice "accidently" landed on the floor right at Faith's nose. She devoured ice until her lips became lined with foam from chomping on her delicacy. In fact, she looked like she had rabies. A wet spot the size of a basketball soon adorned the carpet where she lay.

We had been the first people on the plane but were the last ones off. The airport personnel with the aisle chair were slow in getting to us. I began to get concerned when the cleaning crew started cleaning around us. Maybe we'd be going along on this plane wherever it was headed next!

Finally, airport employees arrived with the aisle chair. Once again, Chas had his hands full while I was transferred to the aisle chair and off the plane, then lifted onto my wheelchair.

"Honey, Faith had a lot of ice on that flight, and we have a layover plus a long way to go," I said. "Could you please see if I can take her somewhere to do her business? Water in, water out."

Chas disappeared. He soon returned with an airport employee. "I'll have to take her. He is going to take me down a set of stairs to the tarmac. There is no grass anywhere for her to use."

"I doubt if she'll go on concrete."

"It's that or nothing."

I relinquished Faith's leash to him and watched the three of them disappear into the crowd. It wasn't long before they returned with Faith trotting by Chas's side. The closer they got, the more she pulled on the leash to get to me. Chas dropped the leash once they got close. She ran to me as if we'd been separated for months. What joy to have someone so eager to be with me.

Less joyful was finding out that Faith had refused to do her business on the tarmac. Boarding our next flight entailed the same procedure with the same results from Faith. At least this time, Chas and I were prepared and knew what to expect. The flight was no different either except that the wet spot on the carpet was larger and wetter. In fact, downright soggy. I felt sorry for my canine partner. Chas and I were served food and drinks, but all Faith got was ice. She didn't beg for food. I was so proud of her. She had to be quite hungry by now.

Time to land. This would be the last time Faith tried to grip the tilted floor with her paws without getting any traction.

"It's okay, Faith," I whispered in her ear, my body too weak to reach over and hold her. "I won't let you fall."

Touchdown. The bump jostled Faith. Her frightened face looked at me as if asking me to make it stop, but she responded to my reassuring words.

Another wait for the airport personnel to transfer me to the aisle chair, push me off the plane, and transfer me to my wheelchair. We didn't have to wait very long this time, but when we got to the place where we were to rendezvous with my wheelchair, it wasn't there. I think Faith knew what was coming because she paced back and forth around Chas, entangling him in her leash.

My wheelchair finally arrived. Faith once again expressed her displeasure during the process. She settled down once I connected her to my wheelchair. She took her rightful place beside me as her signal that she was ready to go. Off we went to retrieve our luggage.

Standing at the luggage carrousel, I pulled out a prepackaged meal from her bag and held the bag in my hand. No dish. Didn't care. Faith scarfed it down. No formalities. I did some calculating and got Chas's attention.

"Honey, it's been over twenty-four hours since Faith ate. No wonder she's so hungry. I would be too. I'm so proud of her. I'm taking her outside to find some grass. I have to use the restroom, but she deserves to go first."

Faith and I headed out the automatic doors into the fresh Alaska air. It took a little searching, but we found the treasured grass for her to relieve herself. Chas caught up with us, lugging all our belongings behind him. Once I used the restroom, Faith and I returned to his side to wait for our ride to the hotel. Our threesome was ready to begin our adventure.

Going without food and drink while traveling didn't keep Faith from doing her job because she loved me. That love overrode her personal hunger. When we are in the midst of a trial or despair, we can continue on because God nourishes our soul. He watches over us and keeps us in his love.

Chapter Seventeen
Faith on a Cruise Ship

E very trip our family took automatically included adaptations for Faith and my wheelchair. Most places are now accessible for wheelchairs but not necessarily for dogs. Once in Alaska, the next phase of our trip was a cruise. Since the ship didn't offer any lush, green lawns, Faith would have to use an oversized litter box to do her business.

When we'd made our travel arrangements, the cruise ship coordinator informed us that a large box filled with pellets would be available for Faith at a particular place on a certain deck.

"Pellets?" I asked. "You mean there won't be any grass? Faith isn't used to doing her business anywhere else. What kind of pellets are these?"

"Just recycled paper molded into pellets," the coordinator explained.

"That shouldn't be too bad," I replied. "I guess I'll have to teach her one more new trick before we go."

I couldn't visualize what this giant litter box would look like, so I called a trainer at *Canine Partners for Life*. "Hi, Megan. This is

Joan. My husband and I are going on an Alaska cruise. They told me Faith will have to use a box for her bathroom. I don't understand. Can you please help me?"

"It's just a wooden box about two feet by four feet and half a foot deep," Megan told me. "That doesn't give a dog Faith's size much room to do its business. Did they tell you what kind of material it will have in it?"

"Pellets made from recycled paper."

"Oh. Dogs don't like those because they are so hard. For dogs, it's like walking on gravel."

"Great! What can I do?"

"Call the cruise line and ask if they can use wood chips. Those are softer and absorb the moisture better."

"Thank you. I'll see what I can do."

The rest of our conversation centered around how to teach Faith to use something so small. Once the phone call ended, I called the cruise line. They wouldn't budge on the material, so the next day I bought some paper pellets and a small wading pool. Now came the hard part.

"Faith, load up."

This was her command to climb into wherever she'd been told to go, whether into the van, a car, or other transport. In this case, the pool. Faith obediently jumped into the pool. But as soon as she felt the pellets, she promptly hopped back out.

"This isn't going to be very easy, is it, Faith?"

The first hurdle was getting Faith to stay in the pool long enough to do her business. Each time she needed a bathroom break,

I led her to the pool and told her to load up. At first, she continued to jump back out. But eventually her bladder made clear it didn't care where she did it. It just wanted emptied.

"Yay! You did it, Faith! You did it! You did it!"

The neighbors probably thought I'd lost my mind using a perfectly good children's pool for a dog, then going nuts with excitement because she peed in it.

Now we had to move to getting her to do number two in the pool. I quickly learned that just because Faith had used her litter box once didn't mean she was willing to use it every time. It got to the point that I tensed with anticipation of a struggle every time she needed to go potty. This made Faith tense as well.

It took more than a week for Faith to regularly use the pool for number one. We were still struggling with number two, and our travel date was fast approaching. As I waited beside the pool for Faith to give up her insistence on grass and do her business, I had visions of my service dog walking around the ship's deck trying to find the perfect spot to relieve herself.

Thankfully, she achieved consistent success shortly before the drop-dead date. I could tell she didn't like it, but she used it. Phew! One less thing to panic about. This would be the first cruise I'd gone on with a service dog, and I wasn't sure how she'd be accepted.

Our Alaska cruise started with a bus ride to the dock. Faith accepted her new challenge of getting on the bus, lying down at my feet, and remaining calm during all the jostling like a pro. I began to relax, trusting Faith to be the superior dog I knew she could be.

If you've ever taken a cruise, you know there are multiple steps once you arrive before you're allowed to actually step foot on the ship and find your cabin. Go here. Go there. You need this paperwork. You need that paperwork. Because the cruise would end in Vancouver, Canada, Faith needed her own paperwork filled out that would permit her to cross over from American territory—Alaska—to Canadian soil.

All this procedure took far longer than expected, and Faith hadn't gone to the bathroom since we got on the bus. Oh, no! There was no grass in sight. Nor could I hurry the process so I could go hunting for her "litter box."

We finally made it to our cabin. Now I needed someone to show me where Faith's bathroom was located. It took what seemed like years before a ship steward showed up to help us. Off we went to Deck 6, starboard side. Finding it seemed easy enough so long as we were following him. I wasn't so sure I could replicate the trek once we were on our own.

As badly as Faith had to go, she wasn't at all sure she wanted to use this box. For one, it was quite a bit smaller than the pool she'd practiced in at home. I could tell she had to go, but lots of sniffing brought no success. We finally went back to our cabin to unpack and figure out our schedule, including dinner since by now all of us were hungry. At least Faith got her dinner in our cabin.

After our meal, Faith and I made another trip to her bathroom. This time she offered no argument about using the box to relieve herself. Number one was easy enough, but number two proved a challenge as the box was so small she had a hard time getting all four legs inside. She finally got her legs inside, but not her deposit. No worries. That's what plastic bags are for.

That was the last time Faith gave any trouble about using the box. Bathroom needs on track, I could now relax and enjoy having her along as my normal companion. Wherever we went, she pushed elevator buttons or any other button needed. She carried packages for me, picked up objects I dropped, and in general behaved like the superior service dog she was. The more she worked, the happier she was. The happier she was, the more she worked.

When we needed to use the elevator, she would stand up and press the call button.

"Wow!" another passenger commented. "She is some dog. Does she push the deck number?"

"No, but I could have her try to push the deck button," I replied. "Then we can see how many decks we get to stop at because of all the lit buttons. Though the emergency button is too close to the deck numbers, so maybe that isn't the best idea. We definitely don't want that pushed."

There were over three thousand people on the ship, and Faith was probably the most famous. Wherever we went onboard, we heard comments such as "I've heard about this dog . . . She must be one amazing dog . . . I keep hearing about all the things she does . . . What does she do?"

In response to that final question, Faith and I performed a mini-demonstration. Pick up my pen. Put my footplates up and down. If a trashcan was close, she threw a piece of paper in it. Plus anything else appropriate for the location and items available. Then I'd have her give the person asking a *Canine Partners for Life* brochure that explained all the amazing things dogs can do.

We began to have some fun with these inquisitive people. They typically asked four questions about Faith: "How old is your dog? How long have you had her? Does she sleep with you? Where does she go to the bathroom?"

To the last, I responded with a smile, "Well, during the last few weeks before we came onboard, I taught my dog to hang her backside over the railing of the ship and do it in the ocean."

Their eyes would widen. "Wow! She sure is a talented dog to be able to do that."

I would then laugh and explain about the litter box. By the end of the cruise, I think everyone had seen Faith perform some kind of task. She had also become quite adept at using her very different bathroom facilities. This had been a most disagreeable new task for her, but she'd refused to give up and had worked very hard to learn it.

All my fretting about Faith not being accepted by the other passengers and crew or getting into trouble evaporated by the end of the first day. I learned several valuable lessons from this adventure. One, good things take time. Two, keep the goal in focus. Three, be willing to progress by baby steps.

Chapter Eighteen
God Used a Smart Phone

The state of Virginia experienced an unusual cold spell while I was visiting one of our two sons, Rory, and his family. Their finished basement provided me a quiet haven to reflect and write.

Unfortunately, all good things must come to an end. My handicap-modified van was packed and waiting to begin our trek home. I enjoyed a last round of farewell hugs from my grandsons. Then my service dog Faith walked up the van ramp and jumped on the backseat. I followed in my wheelchair.

One of the adaptations of my van was a black box attached to the driver's door. It controlled the way the van started, shifted gears, and almost everything else a normal van would have on the steering column and dash. In total, the box had six rows of icons. To move from one row to another in order to select a function, a button had to be pushed. If the van wasn't running, this mechanism had to be turned off or it would drain the battery.

I began my pre-flight checklist. Faith's seat belted. Check. Wheelchair belted. Check. Joan's seat belted. Check. Turn on push-button start controls. Check. Commence ignition. Silence. No engine running.

I started the process over again, only to end up with the same result. *Don't panic. Keep your cool. I have to get home. Must be a dead battery because the button control was off when I got in. My poor van is so old it can't tolerate these cold temperatures. Now what am I going to do?*

On the verge of panic after several tries, I called Rory. He came home from work to rescue his mother. Jumper cables were connected to each vehicle. We were both confident the extra power boost would start my van. I prayed fervently as I once again pushed the start button. Silence.

Giving up on the jumper cables, I called the mechanic in Pennsylvania who had originally modified my van, hoping he might have an easy fix. His response was like throwing ice water on an already frigid predicament. He suggested towing the van from Virginia to Harrisburg, Pennsylvania, so he could examine it to determine the problem.

"Ron, could you please come up with Plan B?" I pleaded. "What if I hang a light close to the ignition wires? Maybe they're just cold. The cost would be exorbitant to tow it that far."

That evening, a small, strategically-placed light warmed the ignition wires like eggs in an incubator. Meanwhile, my son Rory scoured the internet, searching for the cheapest way to get my van home. Every option would blow a hole in our financial pocket. Not to mention all the time Rory would have to spend pulling it behind his car to Pennsylvania, then driving back to Virginia.

The next morning, I made my way across the frozen lawn for a second try. There in the driveway sat my innocent-looking van, an orange tail dangling from its driver's door and weaving up frozen steps to an outside electrical socket.

I positioned myself behind the steering wheel and prayed. My son and his family had emerged into the cold to witness the drama. They all seemed to be holding their breath as I repeated the steps to start the van. Pressing the ignition button, I asked God to please start it so our son wouldn't have to spend his whole weekend driving.

A gentle push of the button rewarded all in earshot with the sound of the engine coming to life. Cheers and praise to God erupted.

Faith and I enjoyed a pleasant, uneventful ride back home to Pennsylvania in the warm van. Relieved to be back, we relaxed from the stress. My van sat in our garage out of the cold winter temperatures.

The next day was Sunday. Chas had a shift that day at the nursing home where he worked weekends as a certified nursing assistant, so Faith and I began our jaunt to church. The events of the previous day still a fresh memory, I was anxious to share the blessing of our answered prayer with others at church. I didn't realize God wasn't finished yet.

As I drove through a sleepy village listening to worship music, my emotional high was interrupted by a sudden loud bang. My brain shifted into crisis mode to determine the possible cause. *Must be a flat tire. How am I going to check for a flat tire without unloading both Faith and myself along the side of the road? There isn't much room to get off the road because of the high grass so close to the edge. Maybe I can check by putting the window down.*

Opening the window, I craned my neck to look down. All the tires seemed okay from what I could see. I spotted a church just a short distance away. The parking lot was filling up, and I spotted a number of people walking into the church. I decided to drive very slowly and see if I could nurse the van as far as the parking lot.

My grand entrance into the church parking lot turned a lot of heads due to the screeching metallic noise now emanating from the van. I scanned the crowd entering the church for anyone who looked like they might help me. *How do I ask someone for help when they are all in their Sunday best clothes?*

I finally called out to a kindly-looking man not far away. "Excuse me sir. Can you please help me? Do you see anything wrong with my van? It sounds terrible. I thought it might be the tires, but they seem okay."

The man walked over and inspected the van. "I don't see anything wrong with your tires, but it looks like you are dragging something. Let me get a closer look." He stooped over to look under my van. "It looks like your left rear shock assembly fell off."

Oh no, God! Now what am I to do? I need Chas! First the cold in Virginia, now this.

We eventually determined that I'd hit a pothole, which had caused the damage. One of the churchmen graciously loaded Faith and me into his car and took us to where Chas was working. He even went inside to find Chas since I couldn't leave the car as my power wheelchair was still back at the church.

Chas came out of the building, looking bewildered. He wouldn't be finishing his shift since Faith and I needed a way home. Back at the church, our kind chauffer helped Faith and me into my husband's car. We thanked him for all his help. After taking a moment to pray with us, he went on inside to the worship service. From the car, I called a towing service, then the mechanic in Harrisburg where my van had been modified to find out if it should be towed to them or someplace else first.

"Well, Chas, at least it won't cost as much to have it towed from here to Harrisburg as from Virginia to Harrisburg," I said optimistically. "We can thank God for that."

When the tow truck arrived, we retrieved what was necessary from my van. Then we watched mournfully as the van was winched onto the truck bed, then exited the parking lot playing piggy-back, leaving us behind.

Everything and everybody were now safely packed into Chas's compact car. We still had one predicament. My power chair sat in the middle of the parking lot, looking like a repentant child who wanted to go with us but wasn't sure how. It didn't nicely fold into a pocket-sized area for transport, so how would we ever get it home?

We began a frantic search of our phone address books, looking for some acquaintance who might have a pickup truck to haul it home. Everyone who came to mind was probably in church and not able to respond to our plea. We texted one person who might be able to help, knowing he too was probably in church so wouldn't be able to answer until after the worship service. I too was supposed to be in church, not sitting in a now-deserted parking lot with my wheelchair beside the car.

"I don't know anybody else who might be available," I told Chas with a sinking heart. "And even if he has his truck, we can only hope he has ramps to drive the wheelchair onto the bed."

My phone was printing a banner across the top with notices of people sending me unimportant messages. I gave little attention, engrossed in the severity of the moment. I was still staring aimlessly at my phone when a familiar name appeared across the top.

"Chas, Kathy's name just appeared on my phone. They recently got a ramp-van like mine. I can text her. Maybe after church she'd be able to take it home for me. I think they pass this way to go home."

"It's worth a try," Chas agreed.

I sent Kathy a text. Shortly after, I received a positive reply. She had people coming for dinner after church, but her brother would take my wheelchair home. All she needed was to know where to put it once he got it to our house.

"That was very strange," I commented to Chas. "Kathy's name appeared on my phone, yet she was in church. Why would she send me a message then? I checked my phone, and there was nothing from her. How did her name appear on my phone?"

Since Chas had made other arrangements to cover the remainder of his shift, we both proceeded on to our own worship service. When we returned home later , my power chair sat right where I had asked. We never saw Kathy's brother pick it up or drop it off.

I asked Kathy about sending me a message that day. Her negative reply added to the mystery.

"If you didn't send me a message, the only way I know it got there was God," I told her. "There was no message from you when I went back and looked at my notices."

God controls the universe, even phone technology. Making someone's name appear on a smartphone was a simple answer to prayer.

Chapter Nineteen
Loss of Power

My forgetfulness cost me time and energy. Energy I didn't have to waste and time that is always in short supply. My wheelchair has a prominently located display that shows how fast the chair is going and how much battery power is left before it stops. There are three bars each of red and green but four yellow bars indicating it's time to think of recharging. I guess the manufacturer knows users need extra warning to replenish its energy.

After many years using my chair, I'd become adept at knowing how many yellow bars could disappear before it was urgent that I recharge. While my body rejuvenated snuggled under warm blankets at night, my wheelchair batteries would replenish with enough power to get both of us ready to travel around my house, run errands, go to doctor appointments, or attend meetings.

One morning, I transferred from my bed to my chair, planning to head quickly toward where most people go when they first awake. The chair turned on, but instead of a full array of colorful bars, the only lights were the three red bars and two of four yellow bars. No green at all. Not good!

"On no!" I exclaimed. "I forgot to plug in my chair last night, and I have a lot of errands and meetings today. Now what am I going to do?"

My stress level rose as I prepared for my active day. I kept glancing at the battery display, hoping more bars would somehow appear by magic. I chided myself for being so forgetful. Unless I came up with a suitable plan to feed my chair's power supply, negligence would cause me to miss an important meeting.

One idea entered my mind. I immediately dismissed it because people would know something was wrong everywhere I went. It would be too embarrassing to keep explaining my predicament or allow people to see the cost of my forgetfulness. I visualized people scowling at me because I insisted on parking myself inconveniently right next to the nearest available electrical outlet.

But this was the only plan that wouldn't leave me confined to the house all day, sulking while I waited for my wheelchair to charge. So I decided I'd just have to endure the embarrassment. Faith and I left the house loaded with my town bag (the one filled with nonessentials you never need until you leave them at home), a briefcase with papers for the meeting, and my wheelchair charger.

Bringing the latter was no small feat. About the size of a car battery and at least as heavy, this rectangular gray box was designed to send power to my chair's two lead-gel batteries.

Struggling to maneuver it from where I kept it plugged into an electrical outlet, I told Faith, "I think this battery charger is made of lead because it feels like it weighs a ton. I can't lift it."

Faith cocked her head to one side as if telling me she had no idea what I meant. She was ready to leave, and I was still struggling with a heavy box that had never gone with us before. She didn't know it yet, but its presence would affect her too.

A new quandary arose. I needed my chair to carry the charger, but the chair was weak because it hadn't been charged. I could only hope my ailing chair wouldn't rebel and shut down when I put it to work. Lowering my footplates to their lowest level, I slid the charger onto them. To keep it from sliding off while we were moving, I raised the footplates to about a forty-five-degree angle.

"Faith, how am I not going to draw attention with this thing between my feet? You'll have to be extra cute today so people look at you instead."

Every time I enter or exit my van, a certain procedure has to be followed. Otherwise, Faith and I get into a tangled mess of leash and wheelchair. Add something else to the mix, and a simple task many people don't think about—getting into and out of a car—becomes a major problem.

I spent the day arriving at meetings, locating a suitable electrical outlet, and plugging in the charger and power chair, only to do it all over again. Even worse, the available charge never seemed to increase.

By the time I arrived at my last meeting of the day, both my brain and body were exhausted. At least I'd be in only one room this time.

Then it registered that I'd have to move around multiple times. Mainly because this final meeting was the local York White Rose branch of Toastmasters International, which met every other week. Not only would I have to go up front to give the speech I'd prepared for this meeting but also to give my evaluation of other speeches.

So much for getting a good charge! Entering the meeting room, I found an electrical socket, plugged in the charger, then plugged its cord into my wheelchair. Sitting back, I watched the display panel show the power pulsing into the batteries. The power my chair had been craving all day.

Unfortunately, I soon had to unplug the cord from my chair to go to the front of the room. Then back to my space to plug in again. Then up front again. Then back to my special spot. I began to feel like an addict in need of my next dose. I had to get back to my charger for my chair to get its next power fix. By the end of the meeting, my personal batteries were in dire need of recharging while my frustration grew with each plug and unplug.

Once back home, I took stock of how many bars were lit compared to when I'd left home that morning. No increase. All the charging I'd worked so hard to do hadn't resulted in any gain in bars. So much for sporadic charging. All that effort just to maintain. If only I'd remembered to charge it the night before.

Disappointment prevailed until I thought, *Okay, no more power but also no less power.* I could be thankful I'd made it successfully through my day without my chair dying completely.

Rethinking my travels while carrying the charger brought to mind the way we treat God sometimes. We pay little attention to our relationship with him until a situation arises where we need his help. Because we haven't been in communication with him on a regular basis, we aren't sure how to talk to him. Will he even listen?

We send up a lame prayer in hopes that something miraculous will happen so we can get out of our problem and on with our life. When nothing occurs, we try again and again, getting more frustrated the longer our troubles persist. Only when we take inventory of our real stance with God, recognize our weakness, and get serious about our relationship do we truly reach out to him. Our attitude then changes for the better because we are now keeping our spiritual batteries charged by keeping the power cord connected to him.

When life loses its power and struggles keep coming, remember to connect to the only power that works—God's power. It's all the power we need.

Chapter Twenty
Milwaukee

I'm hungry," I announced. "Let's stop for lunch. Then we can change drivers."

Chas, our grandson Andrew, and I were on our way to Wyoming. Chas was going to take a wilderness class while Andrew and I visited various tourist attractions. Our drive west was punctuated by frequent stops at different historical sites. Andrew had never been out of the country, so a short excursion into Canada became part of our itinerary. We were coming into Milwaukee, Wisconsin, and still had many hours of driving to get to Minnesota if we were to remain on schedule. It seemed like hours had passed since the last stop, and everyone needed a break, including Faith.

With three passengers, my power wheelchair, Faith, and enough luggage for two weeks, our van was filled to the brim. As usual, Faith had her own suitcase plus a bag full of food to last two weeks and a little extra in case we got detained somewhere.

I was driving at this point. Exiting the interstate, we entered the parking lot of the fast-food chain we'd all agreed on. I pulled into a handicapped parking space, then pushed a button on the black box that replaced the options a normal van had on the steering column and dash. This button should have put the van into park. But nothing happened.

My first thought was that I hadn't done it right, so I repeated the process, making sure I pressed all the correct icons. But the van was still in drive. I guess it wasn't hungry and wanted to keep going to our destination.

"Chas, I can't get the gears to shift. It won't go into park."

"Did you make sure you pushed the right buttons?" he asked.

"Yes. Now what do we do?"

"Pull the hood latch. I'll go check if maybe a wire came loose."

Chas stood in front of the van, his head in the cavity between the running engine and hood. I pushed on the brake pedal with all my might. Visions of accidentally running over my husband sent chills through me despite the hot summer day. I wasn't interested in having my picture in the local newspaper with the headline: "Woman runs over husband in fast-food parking lot."

"I can't see anything. You'll have to turn it off."

"No. If it isn't in park when I try to restart the engine, it won't start. You have to get it into park."

"Well, we might as well eat as I don't think we'll be going anywhere any time soon."

My heart sank along with my dreams of a perfect vacation with our grandson. *I just ruined our vacation because of the modifications on my van. Chas may not even get to his wilderness class. What can we do? It's not like we know anyone in the Milwaukee area who can help us.*

I tried to keep my voice calm as I said aloud, "I guess we get to use our auto club membership."

Because of my disability, we belonged to an organization much like AAA that helped disabled people with vehicle troubles. I made a phone call to ADA (Americans with Disability Act) Roadside Assistance. Within a short time, the representative had sent a tow truck and a paratransit van to take us to a hotel she'd arranged. As we climbed out of our own van, I prayed they could help get us back on the road soon.

Faith had no idea what was happening. All she wanted was to get out of the van, go to the bathroom, and walk around. Exiting the van was easy for me. My driver's seat swiveled so all I had to do was slide from the seat to my power chair. Everyone else had to climb around small suitcases, bags, and souvenirs. Faith had to strategically jump from her seat to the floor close to the exit ramp. Otherwise, she'd land on something not meant to be trampled.

We all made it out safely. After Faith's walk and bathroom break, we joined Chas and Andrew inside to try to get our lunch in before the tow truck and paratransit van arrived. The atmosphere was strained as each of us contemplated what was going to happen. Could the van be fixed? How far would it have to be towed? Special garages that work on handicap-modified vans were scarce. The longer I sat there, the more distressed I felt.

What if the tow truck gets here before the paratransit? We'd have to take everything out of the van and let it sit piled on the ground. If paratransit comes first, then we won't be here to make sure the driver knows where to take the van. I do manage to make everything an adventure!

The headlights of a tow truck shone through the window, announcing its arrival. Chas left his half-eaten meal and all but ran to meet the driver. Sensing the commotion, Faith roused from her spot under the table. We joined Chas outside while Andrew stayed behind to keep our food from being disposed in the trash.

The ADA representative had let us know she'd found a garage that serviced handicap vans only five minutes from where we were. We instructed the driver to take my van there. My van was a Dodge, so I stressed, "Make sure you take it to this address, not to the Dodge dealership."

The driver interrupted my instructions. "Yes, I know where to take it."

I wasn't convinced. Chas and Andrew were in the process of removing everything from the van when the paratransit vehicle arrived, parking beside our van. What happened next reminded me of a circus clown act. Taking turns, one person would enter our van empty-handed and come out with hands full of stuff, walk a few steps, then hand the load to someone in the paratransit vehicle.

I hadn't realized just how many little boxes and bags were crammed into all the nooks and crannies. The paratransit driver gave me a look that communicated his displeasure. I watched as one van became void of its contents and the other vehicle took on the appearance of a moving van rather than one designed to transport people in wheelchairs.

All our material goods were safely transferred. Now we had to figure out how to fit me in my wheelchair, one dog, and two men inside the paratransit vehicle that was already crowded with all our luggage. I had a feeling the driver wouldn't forget this transport.

I'd thought getting us to a hotel and my van on its way to be fixed was exasperating enough. But that turned out to be only the beginning of our escapades. The Milwaukee state fair was in progress, and rooms were scarce. But the ADA representative had managed to find us a hotel room close by with two queen-sized beds, a sofa bed, a small desk with chair, and a wooden cabinet with enough drawers to stash our belongings. By now it was late, and we were exhausted from our trip interruption. We decided to take the next day, Sunday, to organize our possessions so we could find what we needed.

I was stressed about what was happening, and my mind churned with thoughts of how to rescue some part of this vacation that was supposed to be a memorable time with our grandson (it was certainly memorable but not the way I wanted!)

The next morning, we all ventured across the hotel parking lot to a restaurant for breakfast. The grass area between the parking rows displayed old farm implements. I felt right at home. Memories of my childhood watching farmers work their fields took my mind off our van dilemma. An old farm tractor stood sentry at the front door of the restaurant. A tall windmill in the lawn looked like the ones back home that stood beside Amish farmhouses. Its spinning blades turned the wheels on a pump that provided running water in the home. Though relics for show, to me they were a soothing salve for my frazzled nerves.

The rest of the day was spent trying to find and organize what we'd dragged in the night before. Faith gave me a reprieve from boredom as I took her outside for her normal business runs. This should have been a nice break from being cooped up in our hotel room. But the summer weather was so hot I couldn't stay outside very long before my energy drained from my body, turning it into a semblance of a rag doll.

On Monday morning, I was anxious to find out what was broken on my van so it could be fixed and we could be on our way. I called the garage. "This is Joan Patterson. My white Dodge ramp-van was towed to your garage on Saturday. Have you had a chance to determine what repairs are needed?"

To my shock, the mechanic responded, "Ma'am, we don't have a van like that in our parking lot."

"Are you sure? Could you please check? It has a Pennsylvania license plate on it."

"There is no such van in our lot."

Disconnecting the call, I informed Chas that my van had gone missing. My blood pressure rose as my mind began conjuring up what might have happened. Maybe my van really was in their parking lot and they just didn't want to be bothered. Or maybe it was sitting in a junkyard somewhere because the tow truck driver had an accident and my van had been demolished. That was a distressing thought. My van might be old, but it still took me where I needed to go.

After a number of phone calls, the lost was found at the Dodge dealership not far from where it had broken down. It now had to be retrieved and taken to the correct place. By mid-afternoon, it finally got to where it was supposed to arrive Saturday. A day wasted. More time in a hotel that wasn't on our list of stopping points. I tried to control my anger.

"Honey, I specifically told the tow truck driver it had to go to a special garage and not the Dodge dealership. I gave him the right address. It sounds like he didn't even listen. He probably figured he knew better than I did. Grrr!"

Though we had no acquaintances in the Milwaukee area, we were surprised to receive a call from one of Andrew's aunts and uncles. Andrew was our son Rory's son, whose family I'd stayed with in Virginia the last time my van broke down. This aunt was my daughter-in-law's sister. We'd called Rory and his wife to let them know what was going on with their son. My daughter-in-law in turn had called her sister, who happened to live in the Milwaukee area.

The call was quickly followed by a visit. Their company proved a welcome diversion from our misadventures. The men took a drive to see my van and find out what repairs were needed. As mentioned, my van operates through a selection of options on a black box with six different rows of icons. A button moves a display light from one row to another. When it gets to the correct row, I depress the number associated with the icon. The mechanism that moved the light around had broken. The garage had to order in the part, which would take another day before it arrived.

Once again, I tried to hold in my anger. It just seemed everything we tried was going wrong. Ready to vent my disgust, I glanced down at Faith, who lay peacefully at my feet. She'd had her normal routine thrown topsy-turvy. Yet she'd adjusted with no indication of stress.

It was then I reminded myself that bad things happen. God is more concerned with how we react to difficulties than keeping our lives free of problems. We can't necessarily change our circumstances, but we can change the way we react to them.

Taking a couple of deep breaths, I stroked Faith's fur and calmed down, ready to help get us back on the road.

Our van had broken down on Saturday. We finally got back on the road Wednesday with a modified vacation itinerary. We still got to see some amazing sites, and Chas got to his class on time.

Chapter Twenty-One
Flexibility

*T*his special ride didn't start out any different than other unusual ones. Since Faith was always by my side, wherever I traveled she traveled. She got to ride on multiple means of transportation such as train, bus, plane, sailboat, cruise ship, horse and buggy, and ambulance. She wasn't wild about the horse and buggy ride as she was a little unsure about the rumble of wooden wheels on blacktop.

A motorcycle ride was on my bucket list. But a friend who had a specially-made sidecar for her and her dog sold it, so I expected that choice of transportation to remain on my list. One day I was talking with a friend, Frank Herbst, about all the different types of transportation Faith and I had ridden.

"I was hoping for a motorcycle ride, but that didn't work out. Riding in a helicopter and in the cab of an eighteen-wheeler are also on my bucket list. Maybe someday I'll get to try those."

"Did you know I fly helicopters?" Frank commented.

"Oh, wow!" I exclaimed. "Helicopters have intrigued me because you can see the ground you're passing over better than in an airplane."

"I would take you up," Frank offered. "But I don't know about the dog. It might bother her, especially the noise. As it is, helicopter pilots have to wear special ear protection."

"Faith wears doggy earmuffs when we're around loud noises," I informed him. "I could put them on her. Service dogs are trained to accept many different experiences. She's been through so much with me I don't think there's much that would bother her. She is pretty calm even when we're in an ambulance with the siren going."

"Well, the guy who flies with me will be giving helicopter rides at a carnival in a few weeks. If you can come to my house before we leave for the carnival, I'll take you up for a little ride before we go."

"Great. We accept."

A few days later, Frank stopped by. He was carrying something that looked like headphones for listening to music.

"Are you here for our ride?" I asked. "I didn't think it was this soon."

"No, I just wanted to stop by with some ear protection to see if Faith will keep them on. If she won't, she can't go up."

"I'm sure she will. Let's try." I roused Faith from her office bed tucked under the counter. She got up, shook the sleepiness out, and came to my side.

"I have something for you to wear," I told her.

I couldn't tell if her stoic stance was disinterest or she wasn't fully awake yet. I slid the ear protectors over her nose and placed them at her ears. They were much too large.

"Let me have them a minute. I thought I had them small enough, but I guess I didn't." Frank readjusted the ear protectors and handed them back.

I slid them over Faith's nose and covered her ears. "Perfect fit. I had no trouble fastening the strap under her chin. Now we'll see if she keeps them on. Thanks for stopping by and trying them on her."

"No problem. I didn't really think she'd tolerate them. She's a good dog. I'll see you both in a few days."

I was so excited for our flight like a little child waiting for Christmas. Another bucket list item was going to be checked off.

On the morning of the flight, the sky was a flawless autumn blue with few clouds. The fall temperature was perfect for a ride, not too hot that the sun hurt your eyes and not too cold to make a person shiver. As Chas, Faith, and I drove down the lane to Frank's house, I spotted a stately bubble-type helicopter. It was bigger than I'd anticipated. I was glad Chas had come with me to help with Faith and experience the flight with us.

Frank and another man walked us to the helicopter. I didn't want to look like a little kid, but inside I was jumping up and down with anticipation. Then I noticed the height between the ground and the door leading inside the helicopter.

"That's a big step to get in," I said anxiously. "I'm not sure I can do it. And how are we going to get Faith in? I hadn't thought about her or me getting into the helicopter."

A solution was soon found. To get me in, I put my foot on a brace just above the landing rung. Then one person pushed while Chas pulled me in. Once I was seat-belted in and ear protection on, someone picked up Faith and placed her on the floor at my feet. I think her dignity was tarnished. She shook herself, and when she looked at me, her eyes spoke volumes of displeasure.

Everyone was now in. I put Faith's ear protectors on her. She'd been fine when I'd done this at home, but this time she sensed something was different. She didn't try to shake them off, but she did begin to get restless even while lying down.

The helicopter blades began to rotate, and the floor began to vibrate. So far so good. But as soon as the aircraft lifted off the ground and tilted, Faith began to get agitated. She stood up and tried to turn around, knocking off her ear protectors. She wouldn't settle. Her turning left her facing the outer wall, which was basically a rounded, transparent window offering a vivid view of the ground below. This scared her because it looked like there was nothing between us and the ground.

"Sorry for the kind of bird we have today," Frank's voice over the earmuff radio. "We were supposed to have the kind that looks like a long banana. But this is what they sent."

I had no idea who "they" were, but it didn't matter. I was disappointed they hadn't sent the other type of helicopter as I didn't think Faith would be as agitated. Frank worked hard to keep the bird level so Faith wouldn't be so restless. Nothing helped. I tried covering her eyes with my hands, but this only made things worse.

After showing us a few sights, including our home, Frank flew back to his home and landed gently. Faith wanted out *now*. I tried to block the door so she couldn't get past me, but as soon as the door opened, she jumped out. She wanted to get as far from the helicopter as possible, which extended the leash in my hand to its fullest. That didn't bother her. She simply yanked it right out of my hand. She kept on going until an able-bodied man caught her and brought her back.

Faith's helicopter ride reminds me of our walk with God. We willingly follow him just like Faith followed me into the helicopter, lying down at my feet like always. Once the engine started vibrating, she began to get nervous. We do the same thing once our lives begin to vibrate with troubles. Because she could see the panorama far below us outside, she became frantic. All she focused on was the sheer drop outside, even though it couldn't hurt her. We too tend to look at our problems instead of looking to the one who will keep us safe. Once we have a chance to escape, we tend to run away rather than to our heavenly Father, who walks through our problems with us. Thankfully, whenever we are ready to return, he welcomes us with open arms.

Chapter Twenty-Two
Faith's Retirement

Where have all the years gone? It was only yesterday you and I met. An energetic young lady dressed in black fur so shiny you glistened in the sun while becoming invisible in the night darkness. Four paws so disciplined they didn't move unless asked.

You loved to chase a tennis ball no matter where we were or what direction it might take when I threw it. I always positioned my wheelchair in our driveway facing the garage with my back to the road. I wanted to be sure you wouldn't accidently run out into traffic. You would stand staring at the ball with eyes open wide, not wanting to blink for fear you might miss the launch. Eventually, you'd be so tired from chasing the neon-green orb that your tongue hung out and you panted.

"It's getting dark," I would tell you. "We need to go inside. I can barely see you. This will be the last one."

Like a child, you would suddenly have renewed energy and a look of pleading in your eyes for a little more time to play.

In warmer weather, I'd take you where you could enjoy your favorite sport, dock diving. You'd get so excited when I punched in the code for the automatic gate. This opened into a large grassy field fenced on all sides so curious canines couldn't wander away. A medium-sized pond with what looked like a boat dock jutting into it interrupted the flow of the lawn.

You would sit about fifteen feet back from the dock edge, waiting for me to release you for the run. "Go, go, go!" translated to run as fast as you could toward a floppy, colorful floating hot-dog with streamers on each end that I was holding in my hand. As you reached me, I'd released it into the air over the water. Oblivious to the dock ending, you'd jump off chasing your prize.

Depending on whether you caught it in the air, you'd either swim toward your evasive toy or turn your sights toward land, treasure clenched in your mouth. As soon as you reached the shore, you'd run up the grassy slope, flop on your tummy, and chew your trophy. When called, you'd abandoned your leisure spot and race back to me for a repeat performance. This scenario repeated itself until you were so tired you pulled yourself out of the water and flopped on the ground, too exhausted to walk any farther.

"Faith, all done!" I'd call. "Time to go home."

Once again, you suddenly found new energy, and like a child having so much fun, you didn't want to stop. I would give in, and we'd do one or two more rounds before I made you quit.

Traveling included planning and packing for your needs. You had your own suitcase complete with a black dog identification tag.

You relaxed on the back seat of our car as we journeyed throughout our great nation. No matter where we went, you always enjoyed being the center of attention. You loved to show off and would switch into "demo mode," performing tasks to the ooooos and aahhs of your audience. Thirty-seven states and three Canadian provinces got to see you taking care of me.

I will never forget our trip to Rocky Mountain National Park in Colorado. When we arrived at the visitor center, the park rangers encouraged us to drink lots of water because the altitude made our bodies need extra hydration. I remember thinking, *How am I going to get Faith to drink? I can't make her, and she only drinks after she eats. She's getting persnickety about only drinking out of her own bowl. She doesn't like her travel water bowl anymore. But I'll try.*

Thinking I was conducting an act of futility, I removed the doggie travel water bottle and bowl from the rear of my wheelchair. I placed the bowl on the floor and began filling it with water. As though you'd heard what the ranger said, you consumed almost all the contents of the quart-sized bottle.

"I guess she knew she needed to drink," I said to Chas.

When we traveled in my van, you would prance up the ramp, leap onto the back seat, lie down, and wait for me to fasten your two seatbelts. One belt secured your front end and the second one made sure your back end stayed on the seat if I had to suddenly apply the brakes. As soon as the seatbelts were unbuckled on arrival, you'd jump off your seat and strut down the ramp ready for adventures.

You knew me better than I know myself. When I felt sad, you nuzzled me as a reminder of your love for me. When I cried, I would bury my head in your soft coat while running my hands through your fur. Happiness affected you by activating every part of your body. Your tail swished back and forth so fast it made a cooling breeze. I don't think more than two feet touched the ground at any one time. Your ears flopped up and down as you ran back and forth to me in joyous super-speed.

You put great effort into your play as well as your work. When your uniform came off, you became a totally different dog. You were now free to play, and all the pent-up, controlled energy exploded. You chased balls until my arm tired. Because my arms were too weak, you played tug-of-war with anyone you could find. You always won, either out of persistence or strength. People made comments about you being two totally different dogs. One quiet, restrained, and serious. The other wild, liberated, and rambunctious.

My shadow stayed with me for ten years. Then our momentum began to wane. My energy level tapered off and so did yours. Instead of dock diving for an hour, you became winded after twenty minutes. Your mind wanted to keep going, but your body couldn't. Certain movements became harder for me, and they did for you too. I would ponder how to accomplish something due to my limitations. You hesitated before attempting what you once did with ease such as turning on a light switch or giving my wallet to a cashier.

At first, I thought it was my imagination. Then one day you walked to the light switch to stand up and turn it off. You stood looking at it as if trying to talk yourself into standing on your back legs to reach it. Reality shouted at me. If I truly loved you, I would no longer ask you to do what caused you pain. As I wrapped my arms around your once solid-black and now graying body, my tears drenched your fur. You knew I understood.

Ten years is a long time but not long enough to be a part of me. I didn't tell my hand to do things. It just did whatever I wanted. You were the same way. I wouldn't cut off my arm. So how could I cut you from my side? Yet you deserved to retire, not spend your days in harness working for me.

I called *Canine Partners for Life* to ask what procedures needed to be done for you to officially retire. Their response pierced my heart. When other people's canine partners retired, they got another service dog and moved on with life. There was no way I could. You were too special. Even getting another dog wouldn't be the same. You knew everything about me, my physical needs as well as my emotional needs. No other dog would know when I needed them to stay still so I could hug them as long as I needed until my emotions became manageable.

We'd traveled the road to *Canine Partners for Life* often, always for fun times of learning. Now the trip passed too fast as a box of tissues emptied and the trash can filled. You got so excited when we pulled into the drive. You were probably remembering happy memories. We unloaded and walked to the office. *Do I really want to do this? Maybe it's too soon. How am I going to function until I get another dog? Am I sure I want another one? I don't know if I can go through this again.*

Megan, the program director, met us with somber words of understanding. First, the paperwork to sign. Second, the changes in your legal status. You would no longer have public access to places pets aren't allowed.

"You may undress her now and give the harness to us," Megan told me.

No! I want to keep it as a reminder of our time together.

You knew what was happening when I asked you to put your front paws on my wheelchair footplates. Playtime! You had no idea it would be the last time you'd wear your harness. Tears blocked my vision, making it difficult to see the buckles to unfasten the straps. I wanted to hold this moment forever, but you were ready to play. You thought your burden was going to be lifted temporarily. You didn't know your work time was finished, never to return.

When your gear passed over your ears, that triggered your off-work switch. You immediately dropped to the floor. Legs kicked the air while you lay on your back, wiggling like someone with ants crawling up their legs. No sign of aging now!

The tears were now cascading down my cheeks. Dripping off my face, they made large wet spots on my pants. The special bond we'd cemented crumbled. No other person or dog could ever replace our unique relationship. But you were oblivious to the significance of this occasion.

As we headed back to the van, I watched you walk beside me naked. It wasn't right! You should have your harness on or your jammies, the black cape with service dog patches you wore at night. You were only allowed to be naked when playing.

Sauntering up the ramp, you jumped onto the back seat as usual. I suddenly realized that without your harness I had no way to connect your seatbelts. I hugged you while I sat beside you crying. You licked my tears, confused with the situation. You knew it was no longer playtime, but your harness wasn't on. After ten years executing the same routine of getting ready to travel, you couldn't understand why it had changed.

Riding home, you reverted to your panting, stressed condition. I knew then I'd made the right choice. Once home, you'd no longer have to endure van rides except to your favorite veterinarian.

Other acquaintances with service dogs who'd experienced the retirement of their partner warned me I'd grieve just as if a person had died. They were right. A piece of my heart was severed that day, never to be reattached. You and I were still bonded, but it was a different sense of love.

You could no longer go with me when I ran errands. For my first outing, I chose a one-mile trip to the knife-sharpening shop. It seemed an easy beginning since it wouldn't take long. But I made the mistake of looking at you when I left. There you stood at attention just inside the door, ready to come with me. It took every nerve I had not to give in and bring you with me. I cried the whole way there.

"Where's Faith?" the knife sharpener, Greg, asked me.

I couldn't answer until I composed myself. "She is now officially retired, and I can't bring her into your shop anymore."

"You could still bring her," he assured me. "I don't mind."

You mean well, I said silently, *but you're not helping.*

When the house door opened on my return, you were standing in the same position as when I'd left. Your eyes spoke volumes as if asking, "Why did you leave me? I always go with you." We hugged, and I wet your fur once more.

Chapter Twenty-Three
New Partner and Sibling

F aith didn't understand that she'd retired. I'd been instructed not to have her work. She'd earned her leisure time. Maybe it was policy, but no one had told Faith. Though she now had the freedom to do as she pleased, I could tell she wasn't happy. Harness or not, she wanted to work.

If anything dropped to the floor, she rushed over to pick it up. When the clothes dryer finished its cycle, Faith came to attention waiting for the door to open so she could pull the laundry out and give it to me. After ten years of working together, she anticipated my needs before I had the chance to say anything. The look on her face communicated, "I know what you want. I'll do it. Please, may I do it?"

It was as though she read my mind. How was I supposed to break that bond? I knew our relationship had to change, but my heart didn't want to end it. We had a special connection, never to be duplicated.

I hadn't been able to imagine replacing Faith when I drove down to *Canine Partners for Life* to turn in her harness and officially retire her from service. But it turned out to be just one month after her retirement that I left for three weeks of schooling with my successor dog, a male black Labrador retriever named Giles.

Giles didn't know about my special love for Faith. We had to begin bonding with each other. Common sense said it must happen. My trainers said I must. My head said I must. But my heart said not yet.

Though I tried not to, I found myself constantly comparing Giles's style of working to Faith's. Faith had executed any task I asked of her with gusto. A tug command resulted in the object being tugged with great force. In contrast, Giles tugged with just enough effort to get the job done. It seemed like he wanted to conserve his energy.

It was difficult for me to transition to such a different way of doing the same things. I wanted to teach Giles some personalized skills not taught by *Canine Partners for Life* like lifting my wheelchair footplates. Going back ten years in my memory bank, I searched for the instructions I used to teach Faith. But this proved almost impossible.

How am I going to teach Giles to do the things Faith did automatically? I don't even remember what steps I used.

After training graduation, Giles and I started for home to begin our life together. When I'd brought Faith home, she'd had the house to herself. Now I was bringing Giles into Faith's domain. The two of them greeted each other doggy style. During their conversation, they must have made the decision to play so they could get to know each other. One took off at a run to the other end of the house while the other tried to catch up. They took turns being the leader and then settled down to business. Faith remained alpha dog, and Giles knew it.

It didn't take long before they established a brother-sister relationship. One moment, they were the best of friends. The next, they wanted nothing to do with each other. I had to chuckle at the similarities to human siblings.

Having Giles in the house made it even more difficult to convince Faith that she was retired. I'd give Giles a command, and she'd run to my side ready to obey. If Giles hesitated too long to do something, she'd get impatient, pushing past Giles to do it herself. She'd pick up something I'd dropped and give it to me as though telling Giles, "Watch me do it. It's simple."

Old habits are hard to break for dogs or humans. One morning while it was still dark, I needed to get Giles dressed. Chas was still in bed, so I didn't turn on a light. Removing the harness from its stand, I spotted Giles's dark shape standing in front of me, ready to get dressed. After buckling the clasps, I turned around, only to realize that Giles was still sleeping. I'd put the harness on Faith. When I took it back off, she looked at me as though questioning why.

Still, as the years progressed, even the fun things Faith enjoyed doing began to be ignored. She became content to allow Giles to take over instead of rushing to do tasks herself. She now got to sleep on the sofa whenever she wanted. She no longer hesitated when we walked past the van, wanting to climb inside. It was clear she no longer felt compelled to work because I had her successor to help me.

Faith's gradual change of attitude reminds me of how we treat God sometimes. We accept Christ as our Savior and turn our focus on him. We are happiest when we walk right beside our heavenly Father, ready to do what he wants. The more we serve God, the more we know him. We begin to understand what he wants without asking. The more we please God, the happier we become.

But as time passes, we begin to lose focus. We yearn for what we think will be freedom. We shed our work uniform and wallow in the dirt of selfishness. We think it feels good to do what we want. We no longer yearn to be in God's presence. Once we exhaust ourselves in our false freedom, joy is gone. Life is no longer fulfilling. We wander around searching for a new purpose in life.

Once Faith retired, she could no longer wear her work harness and step back into her service dog role. In contrast, we can always step back into relationship with God. He always welcomes us, selfishness and all. He accepts us back the way we are no matter how long we've been away from him. Though of course, he has no intention of leaving us in our selfishness and lack of purpose. Instead, he restores us to a loving walk of service with our Lord and Master.

Chapter Twenty-Four
Open Doors

We have so many routines in life. Make coffee. Use the microwave. Start the car. Our minds move on auto-pilot. So it was with Faith and me. For ten years, Faith and I repeated the same tasks over and over again in the same order. When I asked her to close the bathroom door, she not only closed it but turned on the light as well. When I asked her to open a kitchen drawer, she opened it, waited for me to get out what I wanted, then closed it again without me telling her.

One of the multi-step routines Faith and I did was to open a public door. The long, blue cord with a clasp on one end and a hook on the other came out from its hiding place in the bag on the back of my wheelchair. I clasped one end onto her harness and hooked the other end around the door handle.

"Get the door, Faith," was all I needed to say. She would walk away from the door, bringing the handle with her so it would open.

"Faith, sit." My next step was to maneuver my wheelchair around her, positioning it to hold the door open while Faith went on through. I then unhooked the hook and backed my power chair through the rest of the opening so the door could close.

This may sound complicated, and indeed it is. But after executing the procedure multiple times, Faith and I both knew what to do. All that was needed once I'd attached the cord to Faith and the door was to say, "Faith, get the door." Everything from then on was done without any further prodding from me.

That was Faith. Now Giles was my partner, and we needed to perfect our own routines. It helps if the leading person remembers her new partner hasn't opened doors regularly for ten years.

Giles's original license had been issued by the county where *Canine Partners for Life* was located. Now that he was home with me in Pennsylvania, we needed to get him a new license. Off we went to the county seat to purchase one.

We loaded up into my van and unloaded after we arrived. Giles pushed the plate to open the door into the building, then pushed the button to call the elevator. He'd executed each step so far like a pro. Once we reached the right floor, we then headed to the treasurer's office, where we had to open the door on our own. No push button.

Retrieving the blue cord, I attached it to Giles's harness and the door. "Giles, get the door."

The door opened as Giles began walking away from it.

"Giles, sit."

What happened next looked like something out of a comedy routine. Giles sat as asked and looked at me, waiting for me to do my part. But instead of moving forward to prop the door open with my wheelchair, I sat there in amazement, watching Giles slide across the floor in perfect doggy posture as the door he'd worked so hard to open slowly closed again.

It took me a bit to understand what was happening. Giles weighed two pounds less than Faith. Two pounds doesn't sound like much, but when he'd plopped himself down on a shiny, polished tile floor, it meant his body wasn't heavy enough to hold the door open as Faith's had been, allowing the door to pull him across the slick floor as it closed.

Laughing, I released Giles from his predicament. We tried it again, but this time I had him stand while I backed around to hold the door open. The rest of the routine flowed like we were pros.

Giles sliding across the floor, completely oblivious to what was happening, is a reminder of how we can behave when our circumstances begin to slide. At first, we don't realize we are sliding away from where we should be, but those around us notice. We need to pay attention to our actions. If we begin to see that our life isn't the way it should be, we need to stand up and hook ourselves to the right Person. God will help us pull open and enter the correct doors he has planned for our lives.

Chapter Twenty-Five
A Knight to the Rescue

What are most people doing on a frigid Sunday morning before dawn? My guess would be sleeping. In my warm bed snuggled under a mound of covers is where I would have preferred to be. Instead, I kissed my husband goodbye as he left for his second job at the nursing home. There was no relaxing for me. Our dogs, Faith and Giles, wanted my attention. Specifically, to go outside to do their business.

An extending leash attached to each dog kept them controlled so they didn't attempt to find a new place to make their deposits. Giles's leash was attached to the right side of my wheelchair. I held Faith's in my left hand. My free right hand drove my power chair.

It took some coordination to get the dogs plus my wheelchair through the door, make an immediate left turn, maneuver the serpentine ramp, then go across the driveway to the grass. Faith and Giles each had their special place they liked to sniff first.

The moon must have already set because it seemed exceptionally dark. This made seeing two black dogs and where we were going more challenging than usual.

The dogs both found their special place and made their deposit. I wasn't going to try cleaning up after them when I could barely see the grass where they were. Giving each the command to come with me, I turned around, and we began our short trek back across the driveway. The distant porch light outlined the dogs trotting toward the house. They knew breakfast would be served as soon as they got inside.

All of a sudden, Faith jerked to a stop. Past experience told me her leash had gotten wrapped around the axle of my wheelchair. I could go no further without hurting her because each revolution of her leash around the axle would continue pulling her closer to the wheel. My wheelchair could also be damaged because the axle would act like a fishing reel, winding in the cord and growing thicker with each revolution.

I used the flashlight function on my smartphone to see what needed done to free her. The only thing visible was the leash extending from the wheel straight to Faith. She didn't like being caught like a fish on a line and started panicking. I needed help, but I didn't know how to get it.

"We won't be outside long," I'd remarked to my two four-legged companions before we'd left for the arctic cold. "I'll just slip my coat over my pajamas. My slippers should keep my feet warm until I get back inside."

Now I scolded myself because I was getting colder by the second. The brisk wind bit through my pajama pants and coat. If someone stopped to check whether I needed help, they'd see me dressed for bed, not the wintry outdoors. They'd probably assume if I couldn't dress for the cold, I also couldn't keep two dogs and a wheelchair under control. Which would be embarrassing, but at this point I didn't care. I needed help—and soon!

The more I contemplated how to get the attention of someone driving by, the colder I got. I tried waving the flashlight beam from my smartphone at cars passing by. We live in the country where there is little traffic this early in the morning. Four or five cars passed, but each sped on their way to somewhere. Had they even seen the narrow beam of light? It wasn't very strong.

I began to panic since due to the MS, my body didn't shiver when it got cold. Instead, the muscles became rigid, making movement difficult. *God, what am I going to do? Will someone passing by after the sun rises see two dogs attached to a frozen statue? Help us, please!*

Just as I was visualizing this morbid prospect, I saw brake lights. Were they braking for me or just to make the turn? What if it was someone who might harm me? I didn't know whether to be relieved or frightened.

Then a red long-bed pickup pulled into the driveway. *Forget fear. The cavalry has arrived. We've been rescued!*

A tall, thin man with a short beard walked up to me. "Ma'am, do you need help?"

"Yes. Thank you for stopping. The leash is wrapped around the axle of my chair. I can't see it to untangle it."

"Aren't you cold?"

"I guess I am," I said through chattering teeth. The icy wind blew directly into my face. So much for no one seeing me in my pajamas!

The man began pulling off his hooded sweatshirt but changed his mind and kept it on. Instead, he retrieved a heavy yellow coat from his truck and tucked it around me. It looked like one of those first-responder coats with reflective stripes and thick insulation.

"Are you a firefighter?" I asked.

"No." The man sat down on the cold blacktop to examine the problem. Giles stood in place, watching this stranger who was now at his eye level as though on sentry duty. But Faith took the opportunity to play as she gave the man her doggie greeting of licks and tail wags. He couldn't see the tangle, let alone fix it, while she was thanking him canine style for rescuing her.

I gave her the command to stop. But her face was so close to his that she couldn't resist. Nor could she be unclipped from her leash as that meant I'd lose control of her. Both dogs were tethered by their head halter to a leash, and now one of those leashes was unavailable, so there was nowhere else to attach her.

Unfazed, the man calmly unclipped Faith from her confinement and reattached her head halter to the same leash as Giles. The two dogs stood immobile, not sure what to do, their heads touching like conjoined twins connected at their noses.

The man soon freed the leash from my wheelchair, then put Faith back on her own leash. Fervently, I expressed my appreciation. "Thank you for stopping. I would have called my husband, but he is already at work."

That wasn't very smart. Now he knows you're alone. You've just set yourself up for trouble.

"No problem. I was just on my way for my morning coffee."

"I really appreciate your helpfulness."

"Can you get inside okay?"

"Yes, thank you. I'm fine." Returning his coat, I started for the house. Then I suddenly had an image of him following us up the ramp and into the house to harm me. After all, that's the way it happens in books.

Pausing my progress, I looked back at him. "May I ask your name?"

"Marty," he mumbled.

"Well, thank you again."

The dogs and I hurried back the way we'd come. I was anxious to get inside to safety. On the top tier of the ramp, I pushed the button to open the power door. Then I turned around to make sure the man was leaving. I was startled when I realized he was standing right behind me.

"Just wanted to make sure you made it safely," he said. "Sure you'll be okay from here?"

"Yes, thank you." I steered my wheelchair through the now-open power door. It stayed open too long for my comfort. I wanted it closed for a barrier.

Once inside, Faith and Giles were only interested in breakfast. I was more interested in watching to make sure the man and his pickup truck actually left my property. Then I realized how silly my worries were. I had prayed for help, and God had answered my prayer by sending someone to my rescue. He'd known what I needed far more than I did and had known it before my mishap ever occurred. In fact, this man was already driving for his morning coffee before the leash got tangled.

So why would I ever think that the help God had sent might then harm me? In fact, far from being someone I had any reason to fear, this man had done more than I'd even prayed about. He'd not only untangled the leash but provided a coat to keep me warm. He'd cared about keeping my dogs near me and had made sure I was able to get back into our warm house. When I'd feared I might end up an icy popsicle in my own driveway, God had protected me from harm by sending a chivalrous knight named Marty in a red pickup truck.

Epilogue
Well Done, Faithful Servant

Each year on the fifteenth of January, Chas and I celebrated Faith's birthday. Three Januarys had passed since her retirement and Giles's arrival in our home. At fifteen, Faith was a regal lady, her black hair now thoroughly specked with gray and her muzzle completely white. She began spending more time in bed. Giles checked on her periodically throughout the day to make sure she was okay.

When did they change Alpha dog places? I wondered. *Giles is taking his role seriously.*

We now had to walk Faith down my wheelchair ramp because steps had become too difficult to maneuver. Pain pills and a special joint supplement became part of her diet. She started to look like two different dogs. From her head down through her ribcage, she still had her girlish figure. But her back end looked like an emaciated dog who wasn't being fed. The muscles in her hips had atrophied.

One day while she was lying in her bed, I noticed a lump toward her back end. I touched it and stifled a cry. It was her hip bone! She had lost so much muscle mass that her hip bone was pushing up against her skin. Stroking her sleeping body, I wondered how much longer she would stay with us.

"When do you know it's time?" I asked at a service dog support class.

"You'll know." It was same response I'd received about her retirement.

Then Faith began having trouble getting her back legs to cooperate. They didn't always want to stand.

"Is the floor too slippery today?" I would say to her as I gently lifted her hips.

Faith's two happiest activities were when she was running off a dock chasing her hot dog toy into the water or chasing a tennis ball. Panting hard with her bright pink tongue hanging out, she'd sit in front of me, bright eyes scrutinizing my every move in anticipation of another throw.

Though dock diving was now in the past, she still trotted after her tennis ball when I gently rolled it from the living room into the kitchen.

But eventually, her trot slowed to a walk. Then she began losing where the ball went if it rolled out of her sight. She'd walked partway after it, then stand in one place, not sure what to do. Once I showed her where it was, she'd grab it and bring it back for more.

It's getting close to the time. But as long as she wants to play with her tennis ball, I'll know she's okay.

Early one morning, Faith lay on the rug inside the door after coming back from doing her business. She tried to stand but couldn't get her back legs to work no matter how hard she tried. She gave me the look that said she was tired. Leaning over to lift her legs, I hugged her, my tears flowing.

Faith ate her breakfast and went back to bed. Both dogs fed, their dishes washed and put away, it was time to play. I took Giles's and Faith's balls from the kitchen windowsill where they sat drying from the previous play time. Something inside me said there wouldn't be two balls up there much longer.

Seeing the balls, Giles began racing back and forth from the kitchen to the living room. When called, Faith came to join us for playtime. I always threw her ball first to give her a head start so Giles didn't run her over. It left my hand, rolling across the floor in slow motion. Faith followed it in slow motion. When it came to a stop, she stood over it, looking. Without picking it up, she turned around, lumbered past me, and went back to bed.

No! You have to go get your ball. You have to play. It's not time. I'm not ready. I know I promised myself, but I don't want to keep that promise. I can't!

I reached for my phone, but I couldn't call the vet. Instead, I called Chas. "It's time for Faith to go to the vet. Will you please call? I can't."

"Do you want me to come home from work?"

"No. I'll spend the day enjoying her."

That evening, Faith took her last car ride. Never again would she be frightened and panting as if she couldn't breathe. A good friend, Marian, accompanied us to help keep Faith calm in the car and take care of Giles when the time came.

Once at the veterinary clinic, our entourage filled the width of the hall as we walked from the waiting room toward the special room reserved for these occasions. We had to keep moving, but none of us wanted to arrive at our destination. Chas held Faith's leash, Giles and I following him. We passed one exam room, then a second exam room before Faith walked into the exam room where she'd always gotten to see her favorite vet.

She always goes into that room. For thirteen years, she went into that room. How do I say no to her?

"Not this time, Faith," I said gently. "We're not going in there. Come this way."

She obediently came back out and walked into the special room, never to walk out. A veterinary technician helped us place pillows on the floor so we could be on Faith's level. Giles joined us on the pillows. Faith was in so much pain I couldn't get her to lie down. I could see that she sensed my despair.

"For some time now, the fur on her back down towards her hips has been standing up," I said to the technician. "Why is it doing that?"

"It's from the pain," the technician replied.

We who loved her dearly huddled around Faith, not wanting the vet to appear, yet wanting her pain to be over. When the door opened, Faith didn't even do her normal sniffing to figure out who was entering her territory. The vet sat on the floor with us to explain what would happen.

As the drugs took effect and Faith began to relax, I held her across my lap, her head caressed in my arms. Her pink tongue extended from her mouth as she continued panting. Then her breathing became softer and softer until it stopped altogether. A guttural cry left me as I rocked my motionless four-legged love in my arms.

As Faith was carried from the room, my heart went with her lifeless body. Grief charged in. My happy, energetic partner would never be seen again. Even in all her pain and declining mental abilities, she'd still remained faithful in her love and devotion to me. What an example to follow!

Jesus came into twelve men's lives. At the time, they knew very little about this man, only that each had an urge to follow him. The longer they were together, the deeper their relationship with Jesus became. They didn't understand when he talked about leaving them and returning one day. More and more signs indicated that his time of departure was near.

Jesus walked obediently to the cross. The disciples as well as other followers of Jesus couldn't believe what was happening. Grief engulfed their hearts. As far as they understood, their relationship with Jesus had been permanently severed. They huddled together for comfort. But their grief disappeared just three days later when Jesus made his resurrected presence known to them and others.

We also have no reason to grieve if we are followers of Jesus. He is alive and waiting for us. Are you ready and eager to join him? Are you as committed to being a loving, faithful servant to your Lord and Savior as a loving service dog named Faith demonstrated daily to her human mistress?

If so, then just as Faith rejoiced each time I gave her praise and approval, you can look forward to hearing from your Lord and Savior when you find yourself in his presence before God's throne: "Well done, good and faithful servant. You have been faithful over a little; I will set you over much. Enter into the joy of your master" (Matthew 25:23).

I hope and pray you've enjoyed getting to know my delightful, faithful canine partner as I've enjoyed sharing her story with you. Even more so, I hope spending time with Faith has given you a stronger understanding of your loving heavenly Father, who will never leave you or forsake you and will always be there to help you in time of need. That is, if you have placed your faith in God. Never forget, it's just A MATTER OF FAITH!

About the Author

Career educator, author, and speaker Joan Patterson received a Bachelor of Science in education and business and an associate degree in Bible from Liberty University. She taught in Christian and secular schools for ten years. Diagnosed with multiple sclerosis in 1989, Joan used her knowledge of the Americans with Disabilities Act (ADA) to teach the practicality of handicapped access to construction professionals. While more than three decades of multiple sclerosis (MS) have confined her to a wheelchair, she doesn't allow disability to limit her faith, hope, or joy. Joan speaks to churches, women's groups, children's groups, civic groups, schools, nursing homes, and professional groups, both locally and across her region, communicating passionately the life lessons God has taught her through service dog companions Faith and Giles. Along with writing magazine articles, Joan also shares stories of her journey with MS, faithful service dog companions, and walk with God through her blog on her website. Joan and her husband Chas have two grown sons and six grandchildren. Joan can be contacted for speaking engagements and book events through her website at www.joanpatterson.org.

Made in the USA
Middletown, DE
17 February 2023

25035327R00116